THE RED BOOK OF C. G. JUNG

THE RED BOOK OF
C. G. JUNG
A Journey into Unknown Depths

Walter Boechat

Translated from the original Brazilian edition by
Carolyn Hoggarth

Routledge
Taylor & Francis Group

LONDON AND NEW YORK

Excerpts from *Lament of the Dead: Psychology after Jung's Red Book* by James Hillman and Sonu Shamdasani, *C. G. Jung: A Biography in Books* by Sonu Shamdasani, and *The Red Book: Liber Novus* by C. G. Jung, reproduced by kind permission of W. W. Norton.

Excerpts from *Aion: Researches into the Phenomenology of the Self* by C. G. Jung reproduced by permission of Princeton University Press.

Originally published in 2014 in Brazil by Vozes Publishing House as *O Livro Vermelho de C. G. Jung. Jornadas para Profundidades Desconhecidas*.

First published 2017 by
Karnac Books Ltd.

Published 2018 by Routledge
2 Park Square, Milton Park, Abingdon, Oxon OX14 4RN
711 Third Avenue, New York, NY 10017, USA

Routledge is an imprint of the Taylor & Francis Group, an informa business

British Library Cataloguing in Publication Data

A C.I.P. for this book is available from the British Library

ISBN-13: 9781782204510 (pbk)

Typeset by Medlar Publishing Solutions Pvt Ltd, India

This book is dedicated to Paula, a constant companion
in my personal journey through life

CONTENTS

LIST OF ILLUSTRATIONS

LIST OF ABBREVIATIONS

CW—*The Collected Works of C. G. Jung in 20 volumes*. Bollingen Series. Princeton, NJ: Princeton University Press.

MDR—*Memories, Dreams and Reflections*. London: Collins and Routledge & Kegan Paul.

RB—*The Red Book: Liber Novus*. C. G. Jung. Editing and introduction: Sonu Shamdasani. New York, London: W. W. Norton.

Philemon

From *The Red Book* by C. G. Jung, edited by Sonu Shamdasani, translated by Mark Kyburz, John Peck, and Sonu Shamdasani. Copyright © 2009 by the Foundation of the Works of C. G. Jung Translation 2009 by Mark Kyburz, John Peck, and Sonu Shamdasani. Used by permission of W. W. Norton & Company, Inc.

ACKNOWLEDGEMENTS

I am grateful to all the students in my various study groups for their interest and feedback. An in-depth study of is like a descent into Hades, and this descent cannot be made alone. The exchange of various perspectives and ideas has helped to broach the intricate symbolism of the book.

I would also like to extend my special gratitude to Sonu Shamdasani for his illuminating insights and kind support.

ABOUT THE AUTHOR

Walter Boechat is a medical doctor from Brazil who also trained at the C. G. Jung Institute in Zurich. He is a former member of the Executive Committee of the International Association for Analytical Psychology, and a founding member of the Jungian Association of Brazil (AJB-IAAP), where he gives supervision, lectures, and coordinates training. He is the author of *Mythopoieses of the Psyche: Myth and Individuation* and the translator of the revised Brazilian edition of *The Red Book of C. G. Jung*, as well as many other books and articles. His main interests are cultural identity, race, and inter-racial problems in Latin America, body–mind totality and psychosomatics, and the uses of myth in psychotherapy. He is married and holds a private practice in Rio de Janeiro.

PREFACE

Sonu Shamdasani

30 December, 1913, Küsnacht, Switzerland. In the dead of winter, Jung finds himself in his fantasies in the Libyan desert, and encounters the old Christian anchorite, Ammonius, and finds him reading. At this stage in his career, Jung had done not a little reading, as well recently a voluminous collection of hermeneutical analysis of texts in *Transformations and Symbols of the Libido*, but Ammonius proceeds to give Jung's "I" a lesson in how to read a book:

> Surely you know that one can read a book many times—perhaps you almost know it by heart, and nevertheless it can be that when you look again at the lines before you, certain things appear new or even new thoughts occur to you that you did not have before. Every word can work productively in your spirit. And finally if you have once left the book for a week and you take it up again after your spirit has experienced various different changes, then a number of things will dawn on you.

Ammonius goes on to explain to Jung's "I" that he reads the Gospels to seek "their meaning which is yet to come". In this passage, *Liber Novus*, the book itself in the voice of one its personages, instructs us as to how to read it. I first read this dialogue in 1996, and it has haunted and instructed me, as I continue to labour on *Liber Novus* and Jung's *Black Books*, in the asceticism of scholarship.

Walter Boechat aptly characterises *Liber Novus* as a Janus faced work, pointing both to the past and the future. As a historian engaged in the complex task of editing the work for publication, my gaze was necessarily fixed upon the past: for example, to contextualise the work and its genesis to facilitate its reading. To do this, it is essential to avert one's eyes from the concerns of the present.

Liber Novus presents an unprecedented opportunity for a new understanding of Jung's thought, in particular, the interrelation between his "esoteric" work on his own fantasies, and his "exoteric" scholarly works. At the same time it holds open the possibility for a reinvigoration of Jungian psychology. The former is the work of the historian, and the latter the task of the psychologist.

Once published, the fate of a book depends upon its active reception: how those who take it up will read it, and in turn mediate it to others. Through translating *Liber Novus* into Portuguese, Walter Boechat has contributed to what Walter Benjamin would have called its "continued unfolding" in a new culture, enabling it to find a new community of readers. He has now taken up the challenge of reflecting upon what the book may hold for the future of psychological theory and psychotherapy. In so doing, he has provided bridges between the past and the future of the book, opening paths which are salutary and instructive, and which provide an opportunity for Jungian psychology to begin again, through relinking concepts with the imaginal ground from which they arose, and thereby refreshing them with new sap.

PROLOGUE

"Opening *The Red Book* seems to be opening the mouth of the dead"

—James Hillman, *Lament of the Dead*

The Congress of the International Association for Analytical Psychology (IAAP) is held once every three years. In 2010, the IAAP Congress took place in Montreal, Canada. The association brought together recognised Jungian institutions from across the world, and a large number of analysts from all corners of the globe participated, debating and evaluating new concepts and the theoretical and cultural applications of analytical psychology. One of the most significant—and perhaps long-awaited—participants at the Montreal conference was Sonu Shamdasani, editor of *The Red Book*. Shamdasani took part in two events; an evening conference and an afternoon debate, and was enthusiastically applauded for both. Many of the analysts present had questions for the speaker. Rather significantly, a good part of these questions were preceded by words of gratitude for his valuable contribution to widening the understanding of analytical psychology and its concepts through his detailed research of *Liber Novus*. This surely confirms both the strong impact of *Liber Novus* on the Jungian community and the importance of Shamdasani's work as editor of the book. At the same time, however, this raises an unanswered question: what was the real contribution of *The Red Book* to the understanding of analytical psychology? Has the book had any type of significant influence on current approaches to Jungian clinical practice? These are questions that I hope to answer by the end of this book.

President of the Jungian Analysts of Washington Association and coordinator of the panel in which I participated, Janice Quinn, commented almost in passing that the original copies of the book were being exhibited at the Library of Congress in Washington and had already been a huge success. This was very useful to know, as I was planning to return to Rio de Janeiro via Washington, where I could see my niece and revisit some of the city's landmarks, such as the fascinating National Gallery of Art. I had also planned to wander the beautiful streets of Georgetown, browse its bookshops and immerse myself in its past. After hearing this new information, I immediately added a visit to the Library of Congress to my itinerary. It is one of the Unites States's most important libraries, storing around 147 million documents and images and over 33 million books written in hundreds of languages. Some of the most important documents that are kept there include the original records of the founding of the country and the constitution, containing its fundamental republican principles.

When I arrived at the wide tree-lined area outside the Library of Congress, the first thing I saw was a large banner advertising *The Red Book* exhibition including photographs of Jung, the original copies of the book, and some of its images. The banner could be seen from far away and lent a certain prominence to the exhibition. It had been reported that the opening of the event had been meticulously planned and had included lectures given by internationally recognised Jungian analysts. The exhibition was due to open after the launch of the book at the Rubin Museum of Art in New York, another sophisticated affair.

I believe it to be significant that this careful and detailed exhibition of *The Red Book* was installed in the Thomas Jefferson Building at the Library of Congress, alongside the historic documents drawn up by the founders of the republic. Could this exhibition be a symbol of a wider acceptance of Jung's concepts after a century of their widespread rejection by academia? Could there now be an increased openness to accept the universe of the symbolic and the intuitive? It may still be too early to say, and this book shall frequently return to this matter, but there is now no doubt that analytical psychology has managed to penetrate and develop within many different aspects of culture, a fact that not even the most optimistic of Jung's followers could have imagined in decades past.

I had another memorable experience regarding *The Red Book* when I was attending an administrative meeting for the IAAP Executive Committee in Zurich, where the committee usually meets once a year. The hotel where we met in February 2011 was located close to the small yet beautiful Rietberg Museum, which displays exhibitions dedicated to non-European art—more specifically African and Asian art—with the usual Swiss diligence. According to the organisers, the museum had been chosen to exhibit *The Red Book* in Switzerland due to Jung's interest in oriental art and culture. I walked the short distance from the hotel up a snowy tree-topped hill to find a very well organised museum with an entire section dedicated to *The Red Book*.

It was undoubtedly a magnificent exhibition, and included some of the paintings Jung had produced in his youth, drawings of mandalas, and a range of other creations from the time that he was writing *The Red Book*. I was surprised to see a video in which Jung himself played one of the characters, sculpting the famous statue of the god Telesphorus (whose name means "bringer of completion") in his garden next to the Bollingen Tower. Among the most interesting examples of Jung's work was the statue portraying the phallic god of his childhood dreams, to which he gave the name Atmavictu (meaning "breath of life"). The statue was left by Jung in the gardens of his house in Küsnacht.

More recently, *The Red Book* earned a prominent place at the 2013 Venice Biennale. The theme of the exhibition was *The Encyclopedic Palace*, an imaginary museum that was created to contain the entire knowledge of humanity, from the discovery of the wheel to the invention of the satellite. *Liber Novus* and its images were on one of the main displays, demonstrating the book's cultural importance.

These events occurring across the whole world and the translation of the book into a range of languages point towards the enormous impact this work has had on students and researchers of analytical psychology and the wider public. It is still too early to be able to understand the full extent of this influence. However, the simple fact that some of Jung's most remarkable and fundamental ideas are finally coming to the fore is something to be celebrated.

CHAPTER ONE

Introduction

*T*he *Red Book*, or *Liber Novus* as Jung called it, has become the object of intense curiosity since the publication of his memoir *Memories, Dreams, Reflections* (1963). Jung refers to *The Red Book* in the chapter entitled "Confrontations with the Unconscious" when he describes the crisis he experienced soon after his separation from Freud in 1913. One of the book's appendices refers to *The Red Book* and the meaning it had in Jung's life. While it was being written between 1913 and 1930, copies of the book were circulated within a small group of people in Jung's intimate circle. On some occasions, passages and images from the book were published, some of which appear in the book *C. G. Jung: Word and Image*, for example, which was edited by Jung's secretary, Aniela Jaffé (1979). It contains a section dedicated to *The Red Book* and comments on some of its images. The book did not have any further exposure, as Jung's final decision was not to publish it, although this must not have been without some ambivalence, as in various parts of the book it is clear that despite everything, Jung wanted his work to be known.

Nearly forty years after his death, Jung's heirs gave their permission for *The Red Book* to be made available to the public. This authorisation was given—after much debate—in the year 2000,[1] at the turn of the century and a time of great cultural change. Jung gave the title of *Liber*

Novus to this work, but why? The book is truly original and has an almost medieval appearance, with gothic print and beautiful intricate illustrations drawn by the author himself interspersed throughout the text. These illustrations were an original way of expressing subjective experience that would be hard to describe solely through the logic of language. These were the symbolic tool that Jung used to express the inexpressible content he discovered from the boundaries of the comprehensible. As this book will reveal, images appear at times when logical explanations or descriptions are no longer sufficient, and Jung makes use of this form of aesthetic expression in order to express himself at these moments.

The man chosen to edit the book was the Singapore-born English historian Sonu Shamdasani. Shamdasani is a researcher who has studied the history of medicine and psychoanalysis, and has conducted essential historical research into analytical psychology (Shamdasani, 1995, 2003). The choice of a historian to edit *Liber Novus* (as opposed to a Jungian analyst) emphasises the historical links between the creative experiences contained in *The Red Book*, with the theoretic concepts in the author's complete works being formulated as a result of these experiences. The launch of Shamdasani's exquisite edition of *The Red Book* took place in October 2009. The international response was considerable, and the book was almost immediately translated into a range of languages. In December 2012, the book had already sold over 100,000 copies not only in the original English but in a range of languages, including German, Italian, Spanish, Japanese, Portuguese, French, Czech, and Romanian.[2]

The Red Book was the principal initiative by the Philemon Foundation, an organisation dedicated to publishing the entire works of Jung, and which has already published a number of his other works (Jung, 2007, 2008, 2012, 2014). Research into Jung's unpublished work shows that the twenty volumes published within his *Collected Works* do not include all of his writings. In fact, the volume of his unpublished work is practically double that of the work that has been published to date (the Routledge and Princeton University Press collections of Jung's published works are titled *Collected Works*, not *Complete Works*). Various seminars, letters, communications, and conferences have still not been published, including *The Red Book*. All of this comprises a wealth of material for research into Jung's work that is awaited with great interest.

In a book published a few years ago, Shamdasani (2005) states that the publication of Jung's complete works is essential in order to gain a more accurate picture of one of the founders of analytical psychology. The researcher has studied a range of his biographies and reveals that much of the information provided about Jung paints a picture very different to the real man, distorting perceptions of the analytical psychologist and his work. The publication of *Liber Novus* is part of the movement to seek the real Jung and rediscover the basic premises of analytical psychology.

An impressive video showing the complex editing process of the original work in German carried out by the Philemon Foundation is available on the internet. The first edition printed by the Anglo-American publishing house W. W. Norton then went on to sell out on Amazon. com and other such sites before it had even arrived at the bookshops.

Liber Novus can be considered, without any fear of exaggeration, to be one of the most important book releases of recent times. The revelations contained in the autobiography *Memories, Dreams, Reflections* made a big impact, but *Liber Novus* has made even more of an impression as a result of its rich symbolic content, its sincere confessional-style narrative, and its fundamental role in the genesis of Jung's creative work.

Shamdasani sheds some light on the relevance of *The Red Book* in the genesis of Jung's later theoretical work in his introduction to the 2009 publication. He recalls that the book was completed in the autumn of 1913, by which time Jung had clearly organised a wide range of the theoretical developments that constituted the basis of his ideas. It is worth remembering that at this time Jung had already developed his entire theory of complexes using his word association test. His work in this area began in 1902 at the Burghölzli Psychiatric Hospital in Zurich. At the time he had already developed his entire theory on the psychological dynamics of the neuroses and psychoses. In addition, he had postulated the basis for his theory on psychological types, with his concepts of extroversion, introversion, and the polarity between thought and feeling, although the final version of his typology would only be published in his book *Psychological Types* in 1921. He had even outlined the initial description of two layers of the unconscious: one personal, the other collective and containing *Urbilden* (German for "primordial images" (Jung, 1911). These were the prototype for his concept of the archetypes and their associated images which he detailed in the revised and expanded edition of Symbols of transformation of 1951. It is worth emphasizing that the edition of *Symbols of Transformation* that is normally referred to is found in Volume 5 of the *Collected Works*, which was revised and expanded by Jung in 1951. In this edition, the concepts of the archetypes and their archetypal images can clearly be seen in their final form.

Subsequent creative offshoots that were a direct result of the experiences contained in *Liber Novus* refer to the individuation process—the central concept of Jungian theory—as well as the various mythologised and personified figures of the persona, the shadow aspect, the anima and the animus, and the complex symbology of the self with its abstract representations, such as the *mana* personalities, which in *Liber Novus* are mainly embodied by the magician Philemon, his inner guide. Jung himself stated that *The Red Book* was the basis of his entire subsequent creative process.

The configurations that appear in *The Red Book* were first elaborated in the essay *The Structure of the Unconscious*, published in 1917 as an appendix to Volume 7 of the *Collected Works*. These include: the persona as a form of compromise between the ego and the need for social adaptation; the shadow figure; the personification of content that is not compatible with the conscious but at the same time represents the seed required for the future development of the personality; the anima and the animus, which represent the personification of the opposite gender in the unconscious; and the self as the representation of a central organiser of the psyche and at the same time its totality. The presence of these figures throughout the maturation process of the personality and their guiding role during the psychotherapeutic process are what make Jungian psychoanalysis such an extremely personal and vivid experience.

The book is first and foremost a vivid and candid demonstration of the active imagination technique that Jung systematised to enable a creative approach to accessing the images of the unconscious. *Liber Novus* in its entirety is a constant unfolding of an extremely productive process of active imagination, containing a polyphony of inner voices, creative dialogue with a range of autonomous inner images and the gradual integration of the conscious and the potential of the creative unconscious.

The purpose of this book is not to exhaustively analyse all of the elements contained within *The Red Book*. *Liber Novus* is still undergoing a process of assimilation into contemporary culture. Its impact on the Jungian community and on psychology in general is still being discussed and evaluated. Stanford Drob reflects on the possible effects of the book on contemporary psychology in general (2012), and in 2011 the *Journal of Analytical Psychology* organised a symposium to evaluate its effect on the Jungian community. Some of the conclusions reached are discussed in Chapter Ten.

The purpose here is to raise some select issues of interest, which are significant not just in developing an understanding of Jung's work, but also in shedding light on both the great mysteries of human nature and the new dimension uncovered by Jung and Freud: the universe of the unconscious and the possible ways to approach it.

CHAPTER TWO

The gestation of the book

"My life is the story of the self-realization of the unconscious." It is with this powerful affirmation that Jung starts his auto-biography, *Memories, Dreams, Reflections* (1963, p. 17). The contents of *Liber Novus* give testimony to this gradual process of inner content emerging in consciousness, and how by the author's creative impulse this became integrated and later expressed in his life's work.

Jung's midlife crisis

Jung was in a transitional phase in his life when he started to write *The Red Book* and he needed to reformulate his vision of the world. He had just broken with Freud, a decision that had cost him many of his friendships and the protection of the Vienna Psychoanalytic Society, which in 1913 had already gained significant notoriety across the whole of Europe. Jung was an important defender of this movement led by Freud, and was also the first president of the International Psychoanalytical Association (IPA). In 1909 he left Burghölzli Hospital and his position as an assistant doctor under Doctor Eugen Bleuler, bringing to a close what is referred to as his "psychiatric period" in order to embark upon his long and fruitful creative journey. The end of his relationship with Freud and the conclusion of his teaching work at the University of Zurich soon after were the first of many institutional ties that he would break during his lifetime.

These significant changes gained metaphorical expression in *Liber Novus*, in what Jung named the confrontation between the *Spirit of the Times* and the *Spirit of the Depths*. These are two voices that contradict each other and point out different paths. The *Spirit of the Times* represents institutions, the acquiescence of social groups, the easy adaptation of values imposed from the outside, and superficial involvement with the values of the persona. The *Spirit of the Depths* personifies a new, renovating voice that springs up from somewhere deeper, a powerful summons that urges us to dive into an unknown inner world and travel the long road that has never been taken before. This voice is irresistible and calls those who listen to start new journeys.

This entire process began with an impressive vision that Jung describes in *Memories, Dreams, Reflections* (1963) as the beginning of a time of great difficulty, which he called his confrontation with the unconscious:

> In October, while I was alone on a journey, I was suddenly seized by an overpowering vision: I saw a monstrous flood covering all of the northern and low-lying lands between the North Sea and the Alps ... I saw the mighty yellow waves, the floating rubble of civilization, and the drowned bodies of uncounted thousands ... This vision lasted about one hour. I was perplexed and nauseated, and ashamed of my weakness. (p. 169)

This vision from October 1913 turned out to be something of a premonition, as August 1914 marked the beginning of the First World War, a period of tremendous pain and destruction that left three million dead and uncountable suffering across the whole of Europe. The vision described in detail the borders between the European countries that would soon be covered in the blood and bodies of the men sent to fight. However, given that Jung was going through an intense psychological transformation at the time, this vision should also be understand in terms of its subjective meaning, as it also describes the *internal* revolution that the author was experiencing. Indeed, he was passing through what he would later name the midlife crisis (1928), a moment of existential crisis around middle age when a person's interests are no longer focused on the outside world, love, or professional achievement, and the inner world starts to become more important (this process was known in ancient Greece as *metanoia*—"transformation of the mind"). He was thirty-seven years old at the time, and two of the most significant manifestations of this profound inner transformation had already taken place: his breaks both with the prominent figure of Freud and the psychoanalytic movement in general.

The concept of the creative illness

Liber Novus appeared, therefore, during a time of great change, and it was during this period that the experiences contained within *The Red Book* started to take place. Jung's experiences can be understood to be part of the process that the Swiss historian Henri Ellenberger defines as the "creative illness" (1974). He describes acute psychological crises during which creative personalities pass through a period of introspective isolation, self-questioning, and difficulty in adapting to their daily routine. After this period they emerge invigorated with new ideas, concepts, and truths that can benefit the whole of society. A similar process happened with Gustav Fechner, considered to be one of the fathers of psychoanalysis, who after a personal crisis that caused him to lose his vision came up with his concept of the pleasure principle, probably one of the precursors to Freud's concept of the libido. Freud himself also went through his own creative illness. Confronting issues of incest, parricide, and childhood sexuality during his self-analysis, he started to suffer from fainting spells when visiting his father's grave. These blackouts, which were the symptoms of his creative illness, were the way in which Freud expressed the profound conflict between his subconscious parricidal impulses and his feelings of guilt for the real death of his father. Freud began to worry that he may be hysterical. Freud's fainting, Fechner's blindness, and Jung's altered states of consciousness are cited by Ellenberger as some examples of creative illness.

The term creative illness has been criticised for pathologising something that is not a sign of illness but of health. Ellenberger's term is controversial as it employs two words, one of them relating to something desirable and essential and the other to something undesirable and pathological. I believe his approach to be valuable, as creativity always appears somewhere on the boundaries of the pathological, even though these can be considered to be opposites. This demonstrates a veritable *coniunctio oppositorum*, as Jung would call it, the unity of opposites in the unconscious. Creative types must navigate around the snares of the pathological in the same way that an alchemist would transform lead into gold. *Liber Novus* is a continuous process of transformation between these poles. The limits between creativity and the pathological in *The Red Book* will be described in more detail in Chapter Five. The matter at hand is how much Jung as a person was transformed by the inner process that resulted in the production of *Liber Novus*. In fact, *Liber Novus* can be seen as a form of self-analysis that was created by Jung, in which he was the patient, the method, and the therapist. This intense confrontation with the unconscious would form the basis for his own therapeutic method.

Jung wrote of how this process unfolded (Jung, 2009):

> When I had the vision of the flood in October of the year 1913, it happened to me at a time that was significant for me as a man. At that time, in the fortieth year of my life, I had achieved everything that I had wished for myself. I had achieved honour, power, wealth, knowledge and every human happiness. Then my desire for the increase of these trappings ceased, the desire ebbed from me and horror came over me. (pp. 231–232)

His entire inner world and inherited personality as a man with a strict European education and sophisticated values was being called into question and swept away by the tide. The death of significant symbols, a real-life example of Nietzsche's revaluation of all values, cast a shadow of doubt onto all his previous references. Jung remembered at the time: "I thought that my spirit had become ill" (p. 231). The dramatic nature of the vision that Jung describes took place as he was starting to write *Liber Novus*. At the same time, Europe was descending into the crisis of the First World War. This spontaneous vision took place on a train journey between Zurich and Schaffhausen.

Jung's childhood dreams and Liber Novus

All of these occurrences that took place in the months leading up to the First World War may give the impression that *The Red Book* was a result of Jung's midlife crisis and his break with Freud, among other factors. However, I believe that we should consider the psyche of this creative genius *as part of a process* that spanned his entire lifetime. I would like to suggest that we seek the genesis of *Liber Novus* not in Jung's midlife crisis, but as a part of his preceding psychological development. His childhood dreams and experiences describe the beginnings of a gradual process of development that simply becomes more evident in *Liber Novus*. He had already started to battle with existential questions early on in life, at a stage when the child's ego is still undergoing the initial stages of organisation and has a closer proximity to the symbols of the self that can foretell crises, existential questions, and basic problems associated with the individuation process. The first chapters of *Memories, Dreams, Reflections* give us some important clues to understanding *The Red Book*. In addition, knowledge of Jung's family myths and cross-generational issues may facilitate the understanding of his later work, as Jung's creative work was the theoretical expression of his individuation process: *his work was a reflection of his life*.

In order to gain a more precise idea of how unconscious material was already starting to emerge in Jung's psyche during his early childhood, it is worth remembering that he was born in 1875 in the Swiss countryside, in the medieval village of Keswill in the canton of Thurgovia. At this time, the great modern innovations, such as the car and the aeroplane, had still not been invented. In addition, Jung's father was a pastor in the Protestant Church and he grew up in a very religious family environment. His childhood and adolescence were dominated by religious ideals and he lived an extremely traditional way of life.

In *Memories, Dreams, Reflections* he narrates the details of his childhood with moving sincerity. He also portrays how as a child, the issue of spirituality emerged in his psyche with great intensity yet completely naturally. He developed a special connection with a particular stone, and while he was sitting on it lost in thought, he was overcome with a strange fantasy: was it him sitting on the stone thinking about it, or was he being thought about by the stone? Another interesting passage describes how the young Carl had the habit of keeping a fire lit in a gap in a stone wall at his parents' house. This was his fire, the fire of life and the perpetual flame that must be kept burning forever (p. 33).

A powerful fantasy in which he had two personalities stayed with him from his adolescence onwards. One personality was his younger self that lived his daily life and experienced his insecurities and uncertainties, which he called his personality number one, and the other was a serious old man from the eighteenth century, which he called his personality number two. He also attributed this double personality to his mother, who was obese and protective, and who on one hand was a conventional lady and on the other was strangely unpredictable. Jung felt that he had inherited his mother's second personality, making him very intuitive and perceptive of the irrational side of life. He provided an example of this by recounting an episode that took place at a wedding, where he invented a story to explain an issue he was discussing and it turned out to be an exact life story of the person sitting in front of him. This caused him such a sense of unease that he couldn't finish the story (p. 60).

These examples indicate that Jung felt an early intuition that the unconscious could contain a centre other than the ego, a more nuanced personality that represented a potential unconscious with values different to those belonging to the conscious. These intuitions would play a special role in *Liber Novus*, where Jung used metaphorical representations for this other centre of the personality (later conceptualised in his *Collected Works* as the archetype of the self), which appears in *Liber Novus* as the *Spirit of the Depths*, embodied by Elijah and then Philemon.

The first dream that Jung could remember took place when he was very young, around the age of three or four. In this dream, the young Carl discovers a passageway in the ground in a ravine close to the Presbyterian church where his father worked. Entering the passageway, he enters a room lit with a dim light. In the middle was a type of altar covered with a red cloth where he saw an object the shape of a tree trunk made of flesh with a single eye on the very top. He then heard his mother's voice shouting, "That is the maneater." He woke up terrified (p. 26).

This dream haunted Jung for his whole life and was so powerful that it became the source of many reflections that followed him into old age. This first dream contained the religious and metaphysical issues that were central to his thinking and that formed the nucleus of his personal myth.

Clearly Jung was going through the same process that all children go through in relation to their most significant dreams. Their personalities are still being formed and are in very close proximity to the unconscious, meaning that magical thinking, fairy tales, and myths are still part of their everyday lives. Their dreams often contain intense archetypal material from the collective unconscious.

The universal belief of children in "guardian angels" that protect them at times of great vulnerability is an expression of the proximity of the child's ego to the archetypes, and in this case, guardian angels are a personification of a personal daimon, the guardian spirit.

These great childhood dreams stay with them for the rest of their lives and are connected to their personal myth. The archetypal nature of important childhood dreams cannot be understood at first, and it is only much later that their complex meaning starts to make sense. However, this nucleus of subconscious representation has great symbolic power and reverberates over the years in one way or another, whether consciously or unconsciously. The conscious ego may or may not be able to assimilate this material, but this will affect the person's life regardless.[1]

In his later research into comparative mythology, which intensified during the first years of the twentieth century, Jung noticed the importance of the cult of the phallus in the pre-Christian religions and the ithyphallic gods such as Priapus and Hermes, who represented the fertility of men and women, animals, and the earth. They ensured the continuity of life and the generations.[2] These and other experiences gave the young Carl a sense of otherness during his childhood, making him feel different to his school friends and the adults that surrounded him. At the same time, these experiences were a strong calling towards his individuality and his personal creative process.

The exclamation "That is the maneater" raises the question of cannibalism, which is associated with the foundations of religion. It was just around forty years later, when researching mythology for his book published in 1911, *Symbols of Transformation*, that he started to understand the anthropological and mythological implications of his childhood dream. Chapter 13 of *Liber Secundus* (the second part of *The Red Book*), "The Sacrificial Murder", can also be considered to be a rough treatment of this issue.

The dream of the subterranean phallus god contains many impersonal aspects, and fits into the category of "great" or archetypal dreams. The interpretation that Jung later gives of this dream is that it presented him with a chthonic deity in no way related to the canon of established religion. In fact, the young Carl had always regarded his father's relationship with religion with some suspicion, as the rituals he performed seemed automatic and devoid of any authentic religious experience. He suffered a serious religious crisis during his first communion, and felt sorry for his father whose convictions did not involve any religious authenticity. The young Carl swore to himself that he would no longer participate in that type of ritual.

The dream about the ithyphallic god and Jung's other childhood dreams had a notable influence on the theoretic construct of analytical psychology. For those who have read *Memories, Dreams, Reflections*, it is clear that this theory is inseparable from the personality of its creator. Its themes and methods of approach reflect his unique personality. This is evident in the case of institutional religion. The underworld deity introduces the limitations of the traditional way that the gods are represented. As well as being pre-Christian, this deity relativises the traditional Judaeo-Christian representation of the divinity.

The importance of this dream at the beginning of Jung's life is reintroduced with the publication of *Liber Novus* and the research that resulted from this book. It is known that the final calligraphic copy of *The Red Book* was put together from annotations and unconscious experiences taken from Jung's *Black Books*. *The Black Books* were therefore the basis for the final text included in *The Red Book*. The first *Black Book* contained Jung's annotations on his dreams and fantasies up until 1902. It is known that Jung was also looking back at his childhood dreams when he started writing down his intense fantasies and dreams in *The Black Books* again in 1913. According to Shamdasani, the dream about the subterranean phallus was actually a pre-figuration of the Gnostic god Abraxas, the central figure in *Liber Novus*.

Liber Novus *and Jung's crisis with institutional religion*

Another childhood experience that Jung describes in *Memories, Dreams, Reflections* reinforces the importance that his religious crisis had in his life. On one occasion, at the age of eleven, he was in the main square in Basel on a beautiful day with a clear blue sky. While contemplating the city's religious temple, he suddenly felt the impulse to have a forbidden and threatening thought that he feared would take over his consciousness. The thought continued to haunt him and he had difficulty sleeping, and he was so disturbed that his mother soon noticed there was something wrong. In the end he had no other choice but to gradually let the thought enter his consciousness. He thought about the city's temple, its golden roof, the blue sky, and God sitting upon his throne, and suddenly he saw God defecating on the temple, completely destroying it and reducing it to rubble (1963, p. 50).

This is a surprising and original fantasy to have sprung from the unconscious of an eleven-year-old boy, and it demonstrates Jung's total inability to believe in organised religion and his distrust of his father's values. At the same time, these images portray his need to seek personal, original values so that he could express the transcendental. This representation of a new, renovating deity different to the Judaeo-Christian god can be found in *The Red Book* in the form of the Gnostic god Abraxas.

The association between Jung's childhood dream and the Gnostic god in *Liber Novus* is important, as it touches on the difference between genuine spiritual experience and the dogma of organised religion—a key issue for Jung. According to John Dourley (1990), the theory of religion in analytic psychology rests on three basic pillars: universalisation, subjectivation, and relativisation. Universalisation is the understanding that genuine religious experience does not belong to any particular creed but is part of being human, and that great mystical experiences have universal relevance. Subjectivation is the fact that the experience of the *imago Dei* is subjective in nature. The concept of the external, separate god is superseded by that of an inner god that speaks to us from within. The best example of this inner companion is the *deus absconditus* in alchemy—the god hidden in the depths of the material world or the human psyche. Relativisation is the fact that no creed can claim ownership of or exclusivity to any experience of the divine. These limits are important in defining genuine mystical experiences and establishing that organised religion has no ownership over these.

The presence of Gnosticism in Liber Novus

Abraxas is part of the Gnostic tradition in which gods contain elements of both good and bad, and this was a problem that concerned Jung from an early age. Strictly speaking, Gnosticism was a worldview whose adherents believed in the existence of a demiurge, an incomplete and flawed god that created the physical world. The god of the highest good, or *summum bonum*, represents the upper world that is not connected to the impurities and incompleteness of the material world. Abraxas contains these two opposites. His name reveals the era in which he was worshipped. Abraxas is a contraction of *Abir-Axis*, meaning the "Bull at the Pole", which was probably an age during which the spring equinox, the cosmic new year, fell within the astrological sign of Taurus. He had the head of an eagle, snakes for legs, a shield in his right hand, and a whip in his left. Judging by his representations and symbols, he was a very distinctive deity within the Judaeo-Christian religions.[3]

Therefore, the images that Jung saw in his childhood preceded the important questioning of religion that would find full symbolic expression in *Liber Novus*. These representations still in their germination phase in *The Red Book* were later developed and reached full maturity in Jung's writings in *Answer to Job* and a range of other works dealing with psychology and religion.

It can therefore be concluded that *Liber Novus* was a work in gestation since Jung's infancy and is a symbolic product of his own process of personal development. I consider the tendency to attribute the production of *The Red Book* to his midlife crisis or any other personal dilemma to be too hasty. The book emerged during a moment of crisis, and it is during such times that the conscious has more contact with the unconscious, causing opposites to collide, emotional turmoil to be felt, and synchronistic phenomena to occur with more frequency. In the case of Jung, his personal crisis coincided with the First World War. The appearance of *The Red Book* was a central existential moment for Jung, which emerged from experiences from his past that would continue into the future and appear in his scientific formulations.

CHAPTER THREE

The structure of the book

"I advise you to put it all down as beautifully as you can—in some beautifully bound book ... when these things are in some precious book, you can go to the book and turn over the pages, and for you it will be your church—your cathedral—the silent places of your spirit where you will find renewal. If someone tells you that it is morbid or neurotic and you will listen to them—then you will lose your soul—for in that book is your soul."

C. G. Jung's advice to his client Christiana Morgan, discovered in a 1920 diary entry.

—Shamdasani, 2012, p. 121

Liber Novus contains many journeys that lead us to various characters, confrontations, and lessons. The metaphor of the journey can be found in many tales, in literature, dreams, daydreams, mythology, and alchemy. The *longissima via* described the magnum opus of the alchemist philosophers. The metaphor of the journey can be found in well-known literary works: in Homer's *The Odyssey*, Ulysses travels on a nostalgic journey to his home Ithaca. The idea of the endless journey permeates the entire process of the hero's development. The archetype of the journey can

also be found in a range of contemporary works. The characters created by the Brazilian author Guimarães Rosa are constructed along
journeys through the bleak Gerais wilderness in *Grande Sertão: Veredas*
("The Devil to Pay in the Backlands", 1963).

The structure, organisation, and content of *Liber Novus* have led
some readers to compare it to other culturally significant works, from
Goethe's *Faust* to St. Augustine's *Confessions*, Dante Alighieri's *Divine
Comedy*, Nietzsche's *Thus Spoke Zarathustra*, and *The Odyssey*. Even the
ancient Egyptian manuscript known as *Dispute between a Man and his
Soul*, considered to be the first known example of active imagination
(Hannah, 1981), has been likened to the book. In what way is *Liber
Novus* similar to these works?

The confessional, intimate, and extremely personal character of *Liber
Novus* is comparable to *Confessions*, which was inspired by St. Augustine's
change from a mundane pagan lifestyle to the reflective life. *The Red Book*
also represents an important time of transition in Jung's life: his midlife
crisis. *The Divine Comedy* also starts in the "middle of the day", with an
allegory in which the middle of the journey of life is seen as a time for
reflection (Alighieri, 1980). This can be interpreted to mean the important transition in the middle of our lives. The author of the book, Dante
Alighieri, also has a guide, the classical writer Virgil, and travels with
him in his symbolic descent to the world of the dead full of confrontations. Unlike Dante, who is guided on his journey by Virgil (to Hell
and Purgatory) and Beatrice (to Paradise), Jung has multiple guides, the
main one being the magician Philemon. Dante's *The Divine Comedy* also
uses the old and significant mythological theme of the initiation found
in both ancient Greece and the mystery religions known as *katabasis*,
the descent to the world of the dead leading to subsequent renovation.
Dante descends in order to transform himself and gain understanding.
This is the descent that marks the beginning of the learning process
of the novice. The descent is another of the fundamental themes contained in *The Red Book*. It appears quite clearly in "Descent into Hell in
the Future", the fifth chapter of *Liber Primus*.[1] However, the whole of
The Red Book can be considered a sort of process of descent leading to
renovation.[2]

Nietzsche's *Zarathustra* was a significant influence for Jung, who
read it not long before he started writing *The Red Book*. Zarathustra
speaks through Nietzsche in an impressive prophetic tone. This fatal
identification of the author with his protagonist is clear from the

start with its repeated epilogue: "Thus spoke Zarathustra". Where is Nietzsche, and where is Zarathustra? In Jung's book, however, we find a constant dialectic between the author and his characters. There is a constant process of confrontation, the ethical position of the conscious ego that subsequently takes a stand when faced with the content of the unconscious, which is personified by the various characters in the book. There is no sign of the aforementioned dangerous identification.

The books cited above represent processes of psychological transformation and different ways of confronting the unconscious. In the ancient Egyptian manuscript, the author engages in a dialogue with his *Ba* (soul)[3] when he is feeling depressed, harbouring suicidal fantasies, and is tired of the world. His *Ba* presents him with a way out. Similarly, Jung's soul is a constant guide during his existential crisis, pointing out new ways forward through their dialogue. It even comforts him when he feels weighed down with problems, telling him in a consolatory tone: *"The uncertain way is the good way …"*

Here we see an important characteristic of ancient man that was common to polytheistic pagan cultures: the ability to intensely personify emotions, enter into dialogue with these personified feelings, and get guidance for their daily lives using these images from their belief system. Modern culture has dissociated itself from this intimacy with the natural images that are typical of paganism, a fact considered by many to be an advantage and an example of how our consciousness has developed. This may indeed be an advantage, but it is also a disadvantage, as it represents our dissociation from our basic instinctive roots. One of the basic messages in *The Red Book*, subsequently reaffirmed in many of Jung's later works, is the importance of recovering these lost images in order to promote a more balanced development of the conscious mind.

It is clear that the personification of emotion and the ability to interrelate with the created figures is not exactly the same as a cult of a divinity within the polytheistic religion of a tribal society. Modern man has a totally different worldview to a preliterate society and cannot magically turn back time just because nostalgia implores him to do so. The process of personifying emotions represents the recovery of our ancestral mythological roots that have been lost, yet without losing the advantage to the conscious that Western culture has provided. This is a recuperation of our roots without the positivist, unilateral dissociation of the modern age.

Liber Novus presents us with a new way of writing and a new type of communication with inner images, involving a philosophical and religious density that is original and personal. In this book, Jung intensely confronts his inner images, an experience from which he derives the majority of his later formulations. We cannot consider *The Red Book* to be a traditional psychological text. It is first and foremost a vivid description of a range of powerful internal images with which Jung actively interacts and speaks, seeking with indelible scientific curiosity a more definitive meaning and a more transformative message, providing the final meaning for the conscious ego. The writing down and illustration of these experiences in coloured images helps to unveil the unconscious processes on this journey and leads to their gradual integration. Jung always said that the best way to confront inner primitive emotions would be to give them a shape and some type of aesthetic configuration. This basic postulate is expressed throughout *The Red Book*, as it reveals a constant personification of unconscious material, a dialogue with this content, and an attempt to integrate it.

The medieval appearance of Liber Novus

The originality of *Liber Novus* led Wolfgang Giegerich to comment that it isn't really a book (2008). With its extremely original layout on parchment and medieval illustrations in the illuminated manuscript style, nothing of its kind can be found within contemporary literature. Jung decided to lend a medieval-style format to his text. The front page, the right hand page of an open book, is called the manuscript *rectum*. The page to the left is known as the *versum*. Carefully writing in gothic letters, Jung gave special characteristics to the words as though they were small illustrations. He decorated the first letter at the beginning of each chapter with intricate designs in the same way that can be seen in medieval manuscripts.

The illustrations were done using tempera, which is how medieval altars were decorated before the advent of oil on canvas. The pigments were mixed with water, egg white, and egg yolk, lending the illustrations their extraordinary mystical glow. At certain points along the text it is clear that Jung feels as though mere verbal narrative is not sufficient for him to express his profound subjective experiences. For this he uses his illustrations full of symbolic meaning.

I believe that the strong medieval tones found in *Liber Novus* are extremely significant. On many occasions throughout his autobiography Jung talks about the importance of certain values in the Middle Ages, his identification with medieval spirituality, and, in particular, alchemy. In a text written in 1928, "The Spiritual Problem of Modern Man" (Jung, 1970d), he states rather significantly:

> Modern man has lost all the metaphysical certainties of his medieval brother, and set up in their place the ideals of material security, general welfare and humanitarianism. (p. 81)

It is as though the metaphysical references of the Middle Ages were fundamental for the organisation of Western modern man's collective consciousness. From his time at university participating in the lectures organised by the Zofingia Club,[4] Jung began to distrust the paradigm of modernity with its exaggerated emphasis on science and with a disconnect from nature and instinct. At this time he had already started to defend certain medieval values as necessary in the evolution of the Western collective consciousness, an introverted attitude that was important in the formation of contemporary man's values. An analysis of the Middle Ages demonstrates that without the development of principles defended by scholastic philosophy, cultivated in silent monasteries and by the reclusive practice of alchemy, the Renaissance would never have been possible. The medieval period was an era of introversion in terms of cultural libido, which was necessary in order to develop cultural values and civilising ideals. It was only after this medieval incubation that there was enough psychic energy available for a cultural phenomenon as extroverted, creative, and fundamental as the Renaissance. This transformation began in Italy, later extending across the whole of Europe while maintaining its extremely extroverted character, which manifested itself in the arts and maritime discoveries of the age. This is a significant contrast to the introspective silence of the Middle Ages.

Before discovering alchemy, Jung had some recurring dreams. He relates one of the most significant of these in *Memories, Dreams, Reflections* (1963), in which he discovers a wing in his house that he had never seen before with a library containing "a collection of medieval incunabula and sixteenth-century prints" (p. 194). Jung concluded that this medieval library represented a part of his personality that had been previously unknown to him. This dream represented Jung's discovery of medieval alchemy that would take place a few years later.

In addition to his studies of alchemy, references to the Middle Ages appear at various points of Jung's work. For example, in the first chapter of *Psychological Types* (1970b) he conducts a deep analysis of the opposites described in antiquity, from the Church fathers of the first century, Tertullian (the thinking type), and the opposing Origen (the feeling type), to Zwinglio and Luther. He also performs a comprehensive study of scholastic philosophy with its great opposites of nominalism and realism. (Nominalism defends that universals do not exist, these being just *flatus vocis*, an empty sound, and realism proposes the existence of general concepts, or universals.) Jung remembers that the *esse in re* ("being in reality") of nominalism is opposed to the *esse in intelectu* ("being in the mind") of realism, but that there is no middle term. Here he proposes a *tertio, esse in anima*, meaning "being in the soul". Psychology, the science that would much later emerge from philosophy, is the only way that this *esse in anima* and this inflexible permanence in psychological phenomenon can be accounted for in reality. The fundamental question defended in analytical psychology of the reality of the soul has its basis in Jung's concern with the medieval mentality (Jung, op. cit.).

The elaboration of Liber Novus

Since *The Red Book* is the result of intense personal experiences, it can appear as though it is a spontaneous outpouring of the unconscious or created from sudden inspiration. This is not the case, however. The various layers of *Liber Novus* were carefully elaborated over a period of years. Interestingly, *it* was one of the most carefully edited of Jung's works, as noted in his *Collected Works. Answer to Job* (Jung, 1969d) is just one of his works that was inspired by the period in which he was experiencing what Marie-Louise von Franz refers to as a "type of fever" (1975). This fever ended once he had finished the book. However, Shamdasani comments that Jung carefully revised and edited *The Red Book* according to the following well-defined steps:

1) A collection of spontaneous imaginations noted in his six *Black Books* from 1902.
2) The active imagination period lasting from December 1913 to 1915.

3) The typing up and elaboration of these imaginations after careful reflection.
4) After collation, these notes were sent to close friends to provide their opinion.
5) The production of the final calligraphic edition of *The Red Book* with some modifications and added detail.[5]

I think it highly important that there were other people involved, sharing their opinions and exchanging their impressions with Jung. Shamdasani draws attention to the fact that many of the fantasies begin with the exclamation, "Gentlemen!", which he believes is a clear indication that these experiences were to be shared with other people. This healthy creative extroversion I see as a counterpart to his reflective introversion. His concern for other people's opinion is significant and also emphasises that *Liber Novus* was meant to be published, perhaps for the benefit of all those who are genuinely interested in gaining a better understanding of the essence of Jung's experiences and how his fascinating body of work was conceived. On the contrary, the *Black Books* were written in a more personal style and Jung used them to intimately and directly organise his subjective experiences. This difference in style between *The Red Book* and the *Black Books* is more evident when the two levels of *The Red Book* are studied in more detail.

The two levels of the book

The Red Book has a basic structure covering two planes: on the first we have the basic narrative written in direct and emotive language that describes Jung's experiences with his unconscious. Spontaneous images and symbolic configurations with a high emotional intensity emerge in a whirlwind of strange unexpected impressions. On the second plane, these experiences are decoded in a series of interpretations and elaborations. Dense images are put through a process of deep symbolic and interpretative reflection. Here the language is more detailed and psychological, as the rational interpretation of the conscious mind seeks some type of integration of previous primary processes.

Here we see, in the form of a dialectic, the mental dynamic that Jung referred to as "the two types of thinking" in *Symbols of Transformation* (1911). These are linear thinking, which is rational, typical of the conscious and which seeks to adapt to the external reality, and circular thinking, which is mythological, belongs to the unconscious, and involves the language of dreams and fantasies. The symbols of the individuation process would later emerge through the synthesis of these two types of thinking.

Some critics interpret the Jungian *topos* regarding these two types of thinking as though it were an affirmation that linear or rational thinking, which for Jung originates in consciousness, is superior to mythological thinking, which for Jung originated in the unconscious. In the opinion of these critics, this affirmation reveals a trace of cultural evolutionism in his work.[6] Others believe that Jung's proposal that their thinking can de divided into two types is inadequate, as myths also originate from the conscious and are present in metaphors and parables. I believe that Jung never considered linear thinking to be superior to mythological thinking, and that his entire life's work actually represents a move-ment to bring back the mythological thinking abandoned as a result of the positivism typical of the Cartesian paradigm. Jung uses sym-bols throughout his work in order to re-establish this type of thinking. In terms of the presence of mythological thinking in the conscious, it is worth remembering that *parables* (*para*, "alongside", *ballos*, "throwing", "casting") and *metaphors* (*meta*, "beyond", *phorein*, "to lead") are methods of generating a reaction from listeners through the use of a consciously articulated symbol. The beautiful parables of the New Testament such as the Parable of the Mustard Seed and the Prodigal Son are examples of this use of metaphor by the conscious to achieve a particular purpose. The mythological thinking of the unconscious is spontaneous, original, and totally out of the control of the conscious, which is what gives it its originality.

I consider the integration of these two types of thinking to be of vital importance: mythological thinking permits the spontaneous survival of the experience of original images, and rational thinking is a more conscious mode that attempts to integrate new experiences into every-day life. Reading Jung's irrational experiences that were sometimes completely beyond the expectations of the conscious mind, we can see that rational mind at work, providing rational explanations in an attempt to organise the material so that it is accessible to the conscious. The use of symbols provides a middle ground within this dynamic between the conscious and the unconscious, making it easier to navi-gate between the known and the unknown.

Within this perspective, symbols acquire a central importance in the organic organisation of *The Red Book*, and Jung determines this fact from the very start of *Liber Primus* when he discusses the "way of what is to come". He cites the words of the prophet Isaiah, who talks about the way of the saviour. Jung interprets the saviour as symbolic, as only symbols can open up new paths. In all the *Collected Works*, symbols are presented as a fundamental mechanism between the conscious and the unconscious. A quotation from an alchemical text is cited in the frontispiece of *Psychology and Alchemy* (Jung, 1945): "For those that have the symbol the passage is easy." (See also Shamdasani, 2009, p. 229.)

The two-level structure of *The Red Book* is evident in the encounter with the biblical figures Elijah and Salome. Of all of the characters that interact with Jung, these two have a crucial importance. These two strange personifications appear together in *Liber Primus*, and also at the end of the third part, "Scrutinies". Elijah, the powerful patriarch of the Old Testament, tells Jung that the girl accompanying him is his daughter Salome and that they will be companions through eternity. The meeting with these two figures expresses Jung's basic attitude towards the psychological phenomenon known as the reality of the soul. Elijah tells him that Salome is Jung's sister. She is the biblical character responsible for the decapitation of the prophet John the Baptist. This fact and Salome's demonstrations of love cause Jung great anxiety. "How is it possible?" he asks himself. How can the wise Elijah have Salome as his daughter, who is blind and has feelings of love for him? (p. 246). All of this deeply irrational content demonstrates the incomprehensiveness of unconscious material, although it be at the same time extremely real and effective, as Jung would later repeat on various occasions.

Jung then seeks to form creative associations and make psychodynamic interpretations with this spontaneous material from the unconscious. In order to do so, he uses his theoretical formulations relating to the polarity of psychic content and the concept of compensation. Assuming a conscious logical position, he writes that Elijah represents his thinking psychological function, which is more nuanced and superior, and is represented by a spiritual prophet. Salome, on the other hand, symbolises his feeling psychological function, which is less nuanced and is therefore represented by the daughter of Herodias, responsible for the decapitation of John the Baptist, who is also blind, her eyes covered.

This psychological interpretation does not resolve the question of the reality of the soul, however, which is central in this confrontation with the figures of the unconscious. The figures present themselves as real, from a psychological point of view. Elijah does not accept that he and

Salome are symbols, affirming that this is a rational collocation by Jung that does not do them justice. Elijah and Salome confirm themselves to be real. Here Jung unveils the concept of *psychological reality* that he would later develop in his essay *On the Nature of the Psyche* (1954b) and other work produced during the later stages of his creative process. After the surprising encounter with these two unlikely figures, he begins to expand on the theme and to develop his psychological interpretation. The figures of Elijah and Salome provide extensive research material for the theory of psychological opposites that Jung elaborated in his study of the psychological types. They also provide a connection with the method of historical amplification. Going to great lengths to understand these almost incomprehensible characters, Jung seeks to associate them with historical figures of old prophets accompanied by young women. This is the wise old man and young girl pairing that is also seen in the Greek alchemist Zosimos and his soror Theosebia, the second century Gnostic Simon Magus and the young Helena, and a range of other pairs found in the history of philosophy, alchemy, religion, and fairy tales. These pairs represent the eternal flow of psychic energy within the process of psychological transformation.

Here we see two different ways of relating to the numinous figures of the unconscious, of which Elijah and Salome are representatives. These characters have such a fascinating power over the conscious that they can cause dissociative phenomena to occur that affect the ego. This has two ways of defending itself against this power to fascinate (*fascinans*, "to bind"): rational explanation and this *amplification method*. Rational explanation in this case would be the interpretation of the two characters as representing nothing but the psychological functions of the conscious: thinking (Elijah) and feeling (Salome). Although it may by effective in protecting the integrity of the conscious, I find this rational defence inadequate, as even though the ego appears to strengthen, it produces a certain level of dissociation and a loss of the wealth of values that the unconscious experience brings to the conscious. The second system of defence involving amplification is more inclusive, as the experience involving Elijah and Salome does not need to be completely explained as something "other" (like the psychological functions) but can be understood to be an "interior" phenomenon, this pair from the unconscious just one of the numerous repetitions of the wise old man and young girl pairing that can be seen in fairy tales (the old man who imprisons the damsel on the mountain) and myths throughout the ages.

This second method does not simply reduce everything to a rational formula and does more justice to the irrational character of the unconscious, leaving room for more mystery.

Surprising experiences that are totally devoid of any conscious logic can be found at various points along the narrative. The approach towards Elijah's serpent is another example. As if it were completely subject to the imagination, this serpent passes from Elijah to Jung in the following dialogue from Chapter 21 of *Liber Secundus*, "The Magician":

Me [Jung]: "My dear old man … where is your serpent?"

Elijah: "She has gone astray. I believe she was stolen. Since then things have been somewhat gloomy with us …"

Me [Jung]: "I know where your serpent is. I have her … She gave me hardness, wisdom and magical power …"

Elijah: "Away with you, accursed robber, may God punish you" (p. 324).

I believe this process is fundamental in the dialectic of consciousness with the autonomous power of images. The unconscious has the power to fascinate, yet the dialectic position of consciousness is essential. Someone who is actively engaged in active imagination strengthens his consciousness in the process. The conscious element (Jung) can to a certain extent integrate the energy of the unconscious (the serpent), which was previously in possession by a personification of the unconscious (Elijah).

This rich imagery can be found throughout *The Red Book*, but the interpretative position of the conscious is fundamental. At this point it is important not to identify with the images. It seems to me that the reduction of Elijah's power to fascinate is important within the dialectic process, although the serpent maintains its strength as a symbol of psychic energy undergoing transformation as it passes from the unconscious to the conscious. Jung summarises the broad and complex symbolism of the serpent into three fundamental types: the chthonic serpent, the serpent as a symbol of time, and the serpent as a symbol of salvation—the *soter* serpent (Jung, 2008, p. 217). The serpent that passes from Elijah to Jung is the *soter* type that symbolises salvation, as it represents the psychic energy that is gained by the conscious.

CHAPTER FOUR

Heroism and heroes in *The Red Book*

"There are both heroes of evil and heroes of good"
—François de la Rochefoucauld

The first moment in which the figure of the hero appears in *The Red Book* is in the fifth chapter of *Liber Primus*, "Descent into Hell in the Future". This encounter with the hero takes place after Jung's "rediscovery" of his soul and his imaginary isolation in the desert. Far removed from his everyday life, he starts to fantasise about the descent during which he will discover his most intimate internal processes.

This descent motif, which the ancient Greeks called *katabasis*, was very common in the initiation rituals of traditional societies. The hero needs to descend to the world of the dead in order to undergo renovation, cheat death, and return to the world of the living transformed. This process of descent found in the ancient mystery religions still exists in Christianity with the representation of Christ descending into hell and being resurrected on the third day in a state of *corpus glorificationis*. This process is described in the Creed and is a fundamental part of the Christian belief system. In modern psychotherapy, the archetypal motif of death and resurrection is part of the therapeutic process. Every patient needs to die, descend into his (or her, of course) own personal hell, and hit rock bottom in order to transform himself. This is the only way by which a genuine analytic process can take place, and it is the reason that whenever somebody seeks therapy he maintains a hidden ambivalence. On one hand he would like to undergo therapy and to find his individuality, but on the other hand there is a part of him that resists the process in which he has to die. He is afraid and seeks a whole range of excuses that enable him to avoid diving deeper into his issues: lack of time, lack of money, not the right time …

As we have already seen in Chapter Two, in *Liber Novus* we encounter an unprecedented situation in which Jung is the patient, the therapist, and the treatment. This is a very difficult and challenging condition, and it is under these types of conditions that something new is created, new seeds are sown, and the path to a new theory is opened up. *Liber Novus* was written in an original and creative style that Jung developed in order to work on his inner demons and build a new path for himself. He did this using his creative imagination process and through dialogue with a multitude of inner characters.

The hero must fall

As he descends, the author finds himself in an underground world similar to the world of the dead described in the religious traditions. This is described in *Liber Primus* in a threatening scene with the light of consciousness becoming dim, the frightful noise of shrieking voices, and the water becoming dark. Three visions stand out in this terrifying imaginary environment: the figure of a dead blond hero in the dark water, a thousand serpents veiling the sun, and a scarab floating past. These images appear in small illustrations added to the body of the text.

This is the first representation of the death of the hero in *The Red Book*, and this goes on to be addressed in more detail in Chapter Six. It seems as though one of Jung's previously adaptive attitudes is dying as it is no longer useful and must be abandoned. Although the scarab seems to be a shadowy character, in ancient Egypt it was a symbol of rebirth and restoration, and was thought to push the sun along its course, causing it to be reborn from the darkness. The sun is a symbol of the conscious, and in this scene it is engulfed by thousands of dark serpents in a representation of the dying hero: the conscious must die and return to its deepest foundations to question itself and seek out new paths.

In a striking dream that Jung had in December 1913, the concept of hero that must fall returns, revealing that internal events were inextricably linked to the outside world:

> (...) I was with a youth in high mountains. (...) Then Siegfried's horn resounded over the mountains with a jubilant sound. We knew that our mortal enemy was coming. We were armed and lurked beside a narrow rocky path to murder him. Then we saw him coming high across the mountains on a chariot made of the bones of the dead (...) As he came round the turn ahead of us, we fired at the same time and he fell slain (...) and a terrible rain swept down. (p. 241)

Jung painted the scene of the killing of Siegfried inside the folium of the Liber Novus (see Illustration 1). This is a message that the hero must fall, and this was how Jung interpreted it. In the outside world, rebels were

Illustration 1. The murder of the hero Siegfried.
From *The Red Book* by C. G. Jung, edited by Sonu Shamdasani, translated by Mark Kyburz, John Peck, and Sonu Shamdasani. Copyright © 2009 by the Foundation of the Works of C. G. Jung Translation 2009 by Mark Kyburz, John Peck, and Sonu Shamdasani. Used by permission of W. W. Norton & Company, Inc.

killing heroes and the members of high society who represented them. This dream preceded the assassination of Archduke Franz Ferdinand of the Austro-Hungarian Empire by a rebel in Sarajevo. These violent events would lead to the start of the First World War. In his reflections, Jung was realising that the old values that he held in high regard had to perish. He remarked that he did not particularly admire Siegfried, the famous hero from *The Song of the Nibelungs*, a twelfth century epic based on Nordic mythology. In this case in particular, the hero represented very important conscious values that needed to be abandoned. This is analogous to the confrontation of the *Spirit of the Depths* with the *Spirit of the Times*, whose values Siegfried incarnates. It is interesting that Jung is helped by "a personification of the collective unconscious", noted in his *Black Books* as "the little brown man".[1] This man is a configuration of the psychological shadow that needs to be taken into account when attitudes must change in such a way.

The visions and dreams described in *The Red Book* contain various representations of the confrontation of old values other than the hero who must fall. Jung uses this theme in various parts of the book, describing the intervention of the two opposing principles of the *Spirit of the Times*, which represents the values of the conscious, and the *Spirit of the Depths*, which represents new values. The language of the *Spirit of the Times* obeys the known and expected canon and feels familiar. The *Spirit of the Depths* introduces something completely surprising and new. When Jung is astounded by the death of the hero and sees that this is an enigma that he must resolve at any cost, the autonomous voice of the *Spirit of the Depths* says: "The highest truth is one and the same with the absurd" (p. 242).

While princes and heroes were being sacrificed in the outside world, a hero was being assassinated on the inside. These and other parallels appear at moments that were highly significant for the Western world and for Jung as an individual. These significant coincidences tend to manifest when fundamental changes occur on both the outside and the inside. There was a profound association between Europe's dramatic crisis and the First World War and Jung's internal dilemma. These possible associations between the inner cosmology and the outside world may have also been the seed for Jung's later theories on synchronicity. (See also *On the Nature of the Psyche* (1954b) and *Synchronicity, an Acausal Connecting Principle* (1952b).) This possibility should not be ruled out. During large transitions and times of change the ego is in very close proximity to the unconscious and synchronistic phenomena tend to occur. At the time that *Liber Novus* was being written, both Jung himself and European society as a whole were passing through an intense period of transition, and it is at these times that coincidental and synchronistic events between the inner and outer worlds can occur. However, in order to make this interpretation we must use the concept of synchronicity, a theoretic tool that Jung would only develop much later. At the time of these phenomena, Jung was not thinking in these terms. In fact, he was extremely impressed by the coincidence of his recurring vision of Europe being flooded with bodies and the First World War that followed soon after. He confessed to Mircea Eliade that nobody could have been happier than he was when the war started (Shamdasani, 2009, pp. 201–202). What he meant by this was that when the war started he was relieved that his vision had been prophetic in nature and was not simply a psychopathological manifestation *tout court*.

The little brown man

The role of the little brown man (the trickster) is highly creative in Jung's fantasy. When he appears he does not only counteract an old attitude that needs to be abandoned, but the entire collective shadow of the time that was starting to appear in Europe's cultural unconscious. This is symbolised by the omnipotence of the Germanic hero Siegfried. This fantasy is at the same time personal and collective, as despite all the suffering of the First World War, the Second World War was still needed in order to compensate for all the negative aspects that Siegfried represents, namely the pathological omnipotence that results from identification with the hero.

The problem with the trickster had an important role in Jung's later work concerning the *principle of inversion* and the rooting in the instincts. The trickster is opposed to but at the same time compensates for the excessive spiritualisation of the classical hero, which can lead to a dissociation of his roots and to the sin of pride that the Ancient Greeks called *hubris* (see Brandão, 1991). Jung described the trickster archetype using Paul Radin's anthropological studies of the American Indians (1972). Among the Winnebago tribes there was always a figure that appeared happy at their burials and a figure that appeared sad and tearful at their festive rituals. This primitive and phallic hero could undergo disassociation of parts of the body and could manifest as an animal.[2]

The trickster is an anthropological and archetypical figure, and it is needed by the soul. It appears in various forms and across a range of cultures. Ancient Greece had its hero Ulysses, who was full of tricks, such as his idea of the Trojan Horse. After ten years surrounding the city of Troy, Achilles's pride was not enough to secure a victory, even though he was the strongest of heroes. Only the trickster tactics of Ulysses, the mythological descendent of Hermes (the patron of thieves!) was effective enough to ensure victory. Indeed, Ulysses was the mythical descendant of Autolycus, who was the son of Hermes. According to some versions, Autolycus generated the great trickster Sisyphus, who fooled Tantalus—death himself. Other versions say that Ulysses was a descendant of Sisyphus (Brandão, 1991). In Greek imagination, the trickster hero was the opposite of the idealised classic hero figure.

The trickster appears in many different forms in a range of other cultures, such as the medieval court jester who seems superficial and foolish but sometimes provides the king with great truths. Shakespeare portrayed this in *King Lear*, in which the protagonist is living a life of complete decadence and his kingdom is under the threat of total ruin. It is the court jester (the symbolic shadow figure or trickster) that with his jokes and games gradually makes the king (who represents the principle of consciousness and the model of the ego in the kingdom) aware of his decline. Carnival is the ultimate celebration of the trickster, serving as a period of renovation in which repressed feelings are expressed. The typical carnival figure in Brazil is the *malandro* (meaning "scoundrel"), another trickster figure that is associated with betrayal, theft, and deceit, as well as creativity, as shown in the musical by the Brazilian musician Chico Buarque *Ópera do malandro*. (For more on the *malandro* in Brazilian culture see da Matta, 1978.)

I am elaborating on the trickster figure as I consider it significant that this character appeared in 1913 to help Jung defeat the Germanic hero. The strategy used is sordid and cunning and involves an ambush, a typical trickster's ploy. This fantasy seems to be an unconscious process that was significant in controlling Jung's omnipotence and very high ego ideals, issues that he had to confront within himself at various points along his life. His ambiguity in relation to Nazism, which emerged in force twenty years later and would lead to the start of a war that was to be even more cataclysmic than the previous one, would be a controversial issue for Jung and the Jungian community in general. Did Jung really kill Siegfried in an ambush? Did he really forge an alliance with the trickster? Subsequent events show that Siegfried survived to a certain extent and had to be confronted again on various occasions.[3]

The hero that needs to be saved

Another important hero figure in *The Red Book* is Izdubar, who appears in Chapter 8 of *Liber Secundus* in a much more positive light than Siegfried and is associated with a whole range of other meanings. Jung meets Izdubar when he is heading east on what seems like an endless road in a gorge between high mountains. Jung sees a giant figure approaching in the distance that is dressed like an ancient mythological hero from a tribal society. Jung asks the traveller who he is and the stranger replies that his name is Izdubar and that he has come from the East to understand the people of the West and their customs. Jung reveals that he comes from the West and talks about its cities, people, technology, and flying machines used for long journeys. Izdubar starts to feel weak and unwell as the small being talks in an unknown language using scientific and rational thinking. Izdubar understands the elements of nature, myths, prophecies, and magic. He becomes weak and lies on the ground, fearing he will die. Jung also starts to fear for Izdubar's destiny. Suddenly, the hero becomes smaller and Jung places him in an egg. Jung then starts to chant ancient Vedic Indian scriptures to restore his strength. After some time the hero is cured and reborn in the form of the Orphic god Phanes. The hero can then be taken to the cities of the West in a different form.

This moment in which Izdubar is cured through magic rituals is so mysterious that Jung uses beautiful symbolic illustrations to describe the process. The transformation that occurs when the afflicted god is cured and contained in a reduced form inside an egg cannot be described using rational language alone. Perhaps symbolic illustrations are the only way by which this process can be explained.

Nietzsche famously declared that God is dead. Contrary to this, Izdubar's process of cure and restoration speaks of the assimilation of an ancient god into the symbolic inner space and his restoration to take on a different form, *the symbolic image*. Jung would later write in the *Commentary on The Secret of the Golden Flower* (1957) that the classical gods did not die, but are renovated and provoke a large variety of symptoms that can be seen on the therapist's couch.

The gods have become diseases; Zeus no longer rules Olympus but rather the solar plexus, and produces curious symptoms for the doctor's consulting room, or disorders the brains of politicians and journalists who unwittingly let loose psychic epidemics on the world. (p. 37)

Jung's meeting with Izdubar represents the confrontation between conscious rational thinking (Jung) and unconscious mythological thinking (Izdubar). The various illustrations of this meeting reveal Jung as a small, respectful being compared to the gigantic Izdubar. The hero represents the entire tradition that humanity carries, including all of its acquisitions and lessons learned, stored in the form of ancestral memory in the collective unconscious. Faced with this, the values of the conscious seem small. Even so, the small figure of Jung, with his rational thinking and scientific logic seems in some way lethal to the hero god, who quickly becomes unwell. Here we see a beautiful poetic metaphor for the destructive power that the *goddess of reason* can have over symbolic thinking.

Jung's meeting with Izdubar is one of the most important passages in *The Red Book*, as it talks about the recovery of mythological thinking through the imagination. When Izdubar falls grievously ill and is lying on the ground close to death, Jung becomes seriously concerned with his survival. A radical transformation in the size of these characters then takes place: the enormous god becomes very small and is placed in an egg. According to Gaston Bachelard (1989), changes in size are an essential element found in daydreams. In this case this transformation is from very large (the powerful god of mythological antiquity) to very small (the god in a state of incubation inside the egg). It is essential that Izdubar changes in size in order to survive, or in other words that he changes from being something literal to being something symbolic. The key to this symbol is the way that the god is kept alive. Jung comes from the West bringing technology, rational thinking, and practicality, and the god brings the wisdom of mythology and ancestral experience from the East. The indicated path involves the fusion of both, as rationality should not suffocate the mythological, but shelter it under the mantle of a symbolic tool. The psychology of the unconscious is the way to maintain these traditional symbols.

Another important aspect of this meeting with Izdubar is the use of illustration, which represents a non-verbal approach. Since Anna O.,[4] the fictitious name of Joseph Breuer's and Freud's famous patient Bertha Pappenheim, psychotherapy has been described as a *talking cure*, but during the early beginnings of the Jungian method we see examples of ways towards a *non-verbal cure* or through a range of other expressive techniques. Jung and the authors of the Jungian school always valued the use of non-verbal techniques in psychotherapy, putting emphasis on the use of techniques such as drawing, model painting, and sandplay therapy, which can be used to express unconscious content.

A third important aspect of the encounter with the hero Izdubar is the name of the character himself. Izdubar was in fact the ancient Sumerian hero Gilgamesh from the epic *Gilgamesh, King of Uruk*. The name Izdubar was changed to Gilgamesh in texts written before *Liber Novus* was written, and Jung was aware of this. (For more information on the name Izdubar see Ann Casement's interview with Shamdasani in Casement, 2010.) Why then did he use the name Izdubar? This is yet another confirmation that the range of ancient mythological characters from the Old and New Testament in *The Red Book* are actually personifications of Jung's unconscious material, referred to by Shamdasani as a *personal cosmology*.

CHAPTER FIVE

The limits between creativity and madness

"The God
is near, and hard to grasp.
But where there is danger,
A rescuing element grows as well"

—Hölderlin, "Patmos", 1984

"But the spirit of the depths had gained this power because I had spoken to my soul during 25 nights in the desert and I had given her all my love and submission. But during the 25 days, I gave all my love and submission to things, to men and to the thoughts of this time. I went into the desert only at night."

—Jung, *Liber Novus*, 2009, p. 238

The madness of Miss Miller

In 1911, a little while before having the first inner experiences that would later give rise to *The Red Book*, Jung published *Symbols of Transformation*, which was to be the turning point for his separation from Sigmund Freud. The book was based on the travelogues of a young

American woman, although he never knew her personally. Jung thought that the images and poetry in Frank Miller's journal revealed that she could be schizophrenic, leading him to use the subtitle *An Analysis of the Prelude to a Case of Schizophrenia* (1911). The book was published just two years after Jung had abandoned his position as a medical assistant at the Burghölzli psychiatric hospital. There he had followed hundreds of cases of schizophrenia over years and had noticed archetypical mythological content emerging from these patients, as though their personal psyche seemed to have been invaded by archetypal content. However, Jung's pessimistic prognosis in relation to Miss Miller was mistaken. Shamdasani's research now demonstrates that Miss Miller had been a student of the professor and Swiss academic Théodore Flournoy, and had studied under him for a term at the University of Geneva (Shamdasani, 1990). Miss Miller did not present any symptoms of psychosis. On the contrary, she was a very social and talkative lady, had travelled to various countries in Asia and particularly in eastern Russia, and upon returning to the United States had started to lecture on her ethnological experiences. On her travels she kept a journal of her experiences in which she wrote poems and mythological tales. One of these includes the Chiwantopel hero figure, a character that emerged spontaneously in Miss Miller's fantasies.[1] She also included *The Song of the Moth*, which tells the story of a moth that burns after being irresistibly drawn to a flame. According to Jung, these and the other images contained in the book suggest that they were written while the author was psychologically fragile.

We can see the theme of the death of the hero that appears in *The Red Book* among Miss Miller's images. Unlike Miss Miller, who identified more with the themes of the hero and heroism, in *Liber Novus* Jung takes a very different position as Siegfried's assassin. Aided by a figure of the unconscious, the trickster, Jung prepares a cunning ambush in order to destroy Siegfried, who symbolises the heroic attitude that he needs to overcome. From Miss Miller's point of view, the destruction of Chiwantopel is seen as threatening and terrible, as the ego still identifies with the old heroic attitude even though the unconscious is already calling for change. It is important to remember that the mythological hero dies early and no hero dies an old man, as the phase of old age belongs to the cycle of the wise old man. This is why the renunciation of the hero is so important, as he dies after he has completed his task, leaving the world of the conscious and returning to the collective unconscious where he came from. This is an important teaching that comes from the mythology of the hero.

Madness and renewal in times of transition

I have already commented that Jung was mistaken with his prognosis that Miss Miller represented a case of imminent psychosis. Jung would be wrong once more, but this time *regarding himself*. Upon noticing similar and very intense archetypal images emerging in his mind, including those of Europe covered in an ocean of dead bodies, he began to suspect he was becoming psychologically unwell (see Chapter Two). These feelings and his errors in evaluation are understandable if we consider that the ego is accustomed to the standard orientation of the conscious and its everyday experiences. The images of the collective unconscious that emerge are completely new and can cause feelings of discomfort and foreboding. This phenomenon occurs during times of transition: when the archetype of the self is activated a total renewal of the personality can take place. These characteristics are part of what John Perry (1974) named the "renewal syndrome" of the personality. As these images in the conscious are so intense, the ego when questioned tries to understand them according to its usual references. However, when the conscious can use mechanisms such as archetypical symbols to develop and integrate all of this changing energy, as was the case for Jung, there is a high possibility that the personality will develop as a result. This assimilation of new values from the unconscious is a gradual process and can usually be observed in patients over the space of many years. These intense experiences coming from the world of the archetypes can sometimes threaten the equilibrium of the conscious. This situation is common in adolescents, who are generally going through a huge process of transition. The traditional values that they are taught by their family are no longer sufficient, and they are driven (by the self in search of new existential meaning) to question their old values in search of their own. Minor to serious personal crises can be observed at this stage of life, and these are often spiritual in nature. Archetypal symbols usually emerge in fantasies and what seem to be irrational ideas. This can reach the stage of a significant spiritual crisis, but if young patients are able to integrate the archetypal energy into their conscious, they can undergo significant psychological growth.

Liber Novus, as has already been mentioned, was written at a time of transition during Jung's midlife crisis, the part of the process he called his "confrontation with the unconscious" in *Memories, Dreams, Reflections*. There have been many interpretations that suggest that at the time of this radical experience Jung may have been mentally disturbed or suffering from moments of psychological disorientation that he later overcame. These are difficult questions to answer in full, but they are still very important and should be approached with care.

As mentioned in Chapter Two, "The gestation of the book", Jung's midlife crisis can be seen as part of the development of *The Red Book* only relatively. Although this was an important time of transition, referred to by the Ancient Greeks as *metanoia* (meaning "a change of mind"), it occurs as a result of the accumulation of previous experience and is the expression of Jung's personal myth. But to what extent were the limits between normal and pathological crossed by Jung during his transition? A range of sources discuss Jung's psychological stability during the writing of this extremely symbolic book, and it is important to remember that Jung himself doubted his own sanity at first.

The schizophrenic that cured himself

The English psychoanalyst Donald Winnicott wrote a famous and highly controversial review on *Memories, Dreams, Reflections* (1989). Winnicott argues that Jung was the victim of an early trauma, as according to Jung his mother became depressed and was admitted to hospital, leaving the family home. As a baby, Jung suffered as a result of his parents' separation and developed allergic eczema. Skin disease is known to be a typical manifestation of early disruptions in the relationship between a baby and his primary caregiver. Since then, Jung had problems developing a feeling of unification of the self (his first and second personalities), which he was only able to achieve towards the end of his life! Jung also had difficulty expressing his negative emotions in relation to his parents. His childhood fantasy of God defecating on a church reveals aggressive impulses in relation to his father that were never fully consciously worked through, requiring them to emerge in the conscious in this more symbolic form. Winnicott bases this interpretation on Melaine Klein's object relations theory involving partially and fully internalised objects. Children can only experience the total representation of a complete object during a phase of psychological maturity that comes after what is known as the "depressive position". In fact, according to Winnicott, Jung had a rare case of childhood schizophrenia and later managed to cure himself (p. 484).

In a recent book, Jungian analyst Donald Kalsched provides an important reflection on the issues raised by Winnicott (2013). Winnicott's interpretations are not consistent with the information that Jung provided on his early years in his autobiography. His first memories reveal him to have been very happy, with an almost indescribable sense of well-being and connection to his surrounding environment. The disappearance of his maternal figure seems to have happened at a later stage, after his third year when his sense of identity had already been established. Without a doubt, manifestations of original forces that had not been fully integrated into consciousness can be detected on various occasions, and this took place only later through the writing of *Liber Novus*. Therefore, the writing of this book was a way in which Jung worked through the primitive elements in his unconscious, creating a new therapeutic method in the process. Winnicott's interpretations are therefore wrong, although it should be recognised that Jung sometimes had difficulty in recognising elements of his personal unconscious in certain symbolic manifestations and was quick to assign them an archetypal or prophetic character. The dream about the underground phallus, with all the mythical implications that it contains, possesses natural elements associated with Jung's psychosexual development. The idea of a God that defecates on a church reveals impulses of aggression against his father. Kalsched studied the issue of early trauma in a range of patients and detected the presence of what he calls a personal archetypal spirit, which requires protection during traumatic experiences. He also suggests that early trauma can also open up pathways to mystical experiences of an archetypical nature, and that these can have a transformative effect on the personality. This archetypal spirit also opens up new dimensions of perception and creativity. This was the kind of creative process that also unfolded for Jung.

Inspired madness

There are two passages in particular from *Liber Novus* in which Jung deals with the limits of the normal and the pathological, and how conventional approaches to this problem may be destructive and harmful. The first of these is the description found in *Liber Primus* of a descent into hell in the future, where the author faces his shadows. Here he comments:

> When the desert begins to bloom, it brings forth strange plants. You will consider yourself mad, and in a certain sense you will in fact be mad. To the extent that the Christianity of this time lacks madness, it lacks divine life. Take note of what the ancients taught us in images: madness is divine. (p. 238)

Here we see a clear questioning of the ways in which modernity approaches the theme of madness and the problems that result from this issue not being sufficiently dealt with by the classification systems of modern psychiatry and psychology. Shamdasani adds Jung's words under the guise of a commentary about how madness was dealt with in antiquity, *the theme of divine madness*. He cites the various forms of madness that Socrates mentions in *The Phaedrus*, written by Plato:

> Socrates distinguishes four types of divine madness: 1) inspired divination, as seen with the oracle at Delphi; 2) cases in which individuals, when old sins lead to perturbations, burst forth as prophecies and incite prayer and worship; 3) possession by the Muses—the man of technique untouched by the madness of the Muses will never be a good poet; 4) the lover. (p. 238)

He also cites the humanist Erasmus of Rotterdam, who in his essay *Eloge de la Folie* (In Praise of Folly) mentions two types of madness, the madness of men and inspired madness (Erasmus, 1511). The latter is transcendental and divine in nature, and was also recognised by Christianity.

This comment refers to the altered states of consciousness that were evoked in Ancient Greece, and these were seen as existing within the parameters of creativity. The madness of the Pythia (religious inspiration), of man during the creative process (inspired by a Muse) and the lover do not fit within the strict limits of normality as described by modern science. Jung uses transcultural comparison to demonstrate that our definition of normality does not make sense. So-called madness was held as sacred in antiquity, and the creative man inspired by the Muse is also outside what is considered to be normal, as were the attendants of Dionysus, who were impassioned by wine. These are just some forms of creative madness.

"Normality is an ideal fiction"

If the concept of madness itself can be called into question, the parallel concept of normality may also be reconsidered. To cite just one example, Sigmund Freud himself claimed that "normality is an ideal fiction" (1937c). Other writers have worked with the problem of excessive normality and adaptation to collective norms, this in itself being pathological. The well-known psychoanalyst and psychosomatic therapist Joyce McDougall coined the term *normopathy* to describe excessive attachment to social norms and conventional normality. *Normopaths* pay for their rituals of adaptation with an excessive tendency towards somatisation. Symptoms appear less in the psyche and they tend to be observed in the body. The term *normotic*, coined by the English psychoanalyst Christopher Bollas, has a similar meaning. James Hillman (1975) defends that *pathologising* is a spontaneous movement of the soul and a vital necessity of psychic life. The life of the soul includes pathologising, but this is not a serious deviation from a type of normality that is impossible to achieve. The word pathology derives from *pathos*, meaning "passion". The soul pathologises as this is one of its vital movements and basic manifestations. Hillman invites us to shine a new light on psychopathology, in which *pathologising* is a necessary manifestation of the soul that will always be present. Its total absence would be a type of serious psychic anaemia, which would be a symptom of something serious.

Similarly, Jung sought to present the extraordinary, the strange, and the unusual as a fundamental part of human experience, and something new to be incorporated, integrated, and understood by the conscious.

In relation to the problem of adaptation, Jung developed his concept of the persona, a psychological artifice that we wish to show to others (1928, in particular Chapter 3, "The Persona as a Segment of the Collective Psyche"). This social mask is a segment of the collective psyche, and although it is necessary for our adaptation, if used to excess it may provoke problems that will be discussed later. The persona (word derived from *sonare* meaning "sound" and *per* meaning "through") was in fact a theatrical mask used by actors in antiquity. Classical Greek theatre, as a sacred ritual, was prohibited to women, and men had to play both the male and female roles using large masks. We still use these today, and our everyday lives are like a masked play on a large stage. The risk of identifying with the persona and creating a dangerous fusion between our identity and our social masks is substantial.[2]

A symbolic balance

The above demonstrates how difficult it is to evaluate and make value judgements on Jung's psychological state during the years he wrote *The Red Book*. The creative man, at times of *metanoia* ("a change of mind"), goes through a radical transformation of his conscious processes. It should also be emphasised that Jung himself continues to discuss the theme of diagnosing madness in Chapter 6 as follows:

> It is unquestionable: if you enter into the world of the soul, you are like a madman, and a doctor would consider you to be sick. What I see here can be seen as sickness, but no one can see it as sickness more than I do.
>
> This is how I overcame madness. If you do not know what divine madness is, suspend judgement and wait for the fruits.
>
> Speak then of sick delusion, when the spirit of the depths … forces a man to speak in tongues instead of in human speech, and makes him believe that he himself is the spirit of the depths. But also speak of sick delusion, when the spirit of this time … forces him to see only the surface, to deny the spirit of the depths and to take himself the spirit of the times. The spirit of this time is ungodly; the spirit of the depths is ungodly; balance is godly. (p. 238)

Jung makes it clear in the first citation that he understands well that whoever enters into the world of the soul seems like a madman. Therefore, there is nobody as qualified as him, who has actually been through this experience, to say whether this is true or not. In the second citation, Jung uses a lyrical style to suggest that there are two types of madness. In the first, the person feels that he has been taken over by a transpersonal power and undergoes a process of omnipotent iden-tification with the archetype, or a "psychic inflation". In the second, the person feels as though he is the spokesperson of something that is applicable to everybody, and he undergoes a process of identification with a value of the persona. These are both forms of madness, as they are both equally one-sided. Jung uses the balance as a metaphor to say that only balance is divine. He describes that the image of balanced scales was something he lived by. For twenty-five nights in the desert he listens to his soul and the voices of his unconscious. For the twenty-five days he was taking care of worldly matters. This is a poetic way of describing the search for a balance between the world of the unconscious and everyday obligations. This symbolism is used to describe a fundamental factor in the diagnosis of either normality or pathology: the presence of pragmatism. This is the ability to maintain a link with the people and tasks of our everyday lives, with "worldly matters being taken care of for twenty-five days".

A dream about incubation on three levels

Jung returns to the matter of madness in *Liber Secundus*, particulatly from Chapter 15, "Nox Secunda". In this part of the book, Jung imagines himself entering a large library and talking to a librarian, whom he describes as a cultured man who is extremely rational and limited in his logic. The librarian gives him a copy of *The Imitation of Christ*, a medieval breviary on spirituality attributed to the monk Thomas à Kempis. The librarian is unable to understand the spiritual dimension of the book. Later Jung enters a mysterious kitchen belonging to the library. There he has a strange conversation with a cook, who immediately and intuitively understands the spiritual importance of Kempis's book. She even owns an identical copy that was given to her by her mother. Talking to the cook, Jung unintentionally falls asleep and goes through an experience that he considers to be an incubation[3] dream similar to those described in the temples of the god of medicine, Asclepius, in Ancient Greece. Jung calls this an incubation dream as it describes a complex experience that unfolds on three different levels: in the first he is sleeping in the kitchen holding *The Imitation of Christ*; in the second he suffers a psychiatric internment and the limits of normality, creativity, madness, and religious experiences are discussed; and on the third level he watches an elaborate play, in which elements of the legend of the Holy Grail are acted out on a stage. The elements of these three levels explain and correspond to one another in differing degrees. The "dream within a dream" structure is being used here, with each level demonstrating a higher degree of complexity than the last and hinting at a possible interpretation of the entire content of the dream.

In the library with the librarian, his lack of intellectuality is juxtaposed with a genuine search for knowledge. The librarian is surrounded by books but has no interest in *The Imitation of Christ*, a medieval book on compassion. It seems that the cook has a deeper emotional understanding of the book. The thinking-feeling dichotomy and the bias towards reason in Western culture that are discussed by Jung at various points in his work seem to be put into question here.

When Jung is leaving the kitchen, he describes an experience with the dead that are going to Jerusalem to pray at the most sacred of all tombs (p. 294). The cook sees Jung while he is talking with one of the dead and thinks he is behaving strangely, offering him help. The librarian also sees him, and he has a more drastic response, calling the police. Here an allegory is used to describe the conflict between the direct involvement with the unconscious with everyday social judgement, which is unable to grasp subjective events at any level. This understanding can only be obtained through personal experience, which must then be assimilated by the ego and integrated in a socially acceptable way. Perhaps the seed of creativity resides precisely here: the shift of the eternal truths of the unconscious into the realm of the socially acceptable. Madness would be the inability to achieve this shift, represented by the crystallisation caused by the stony gaze of Medusa, the *vitrificatio* ("vitrification") of the alchemical *albedo* frozen into rigid images.

In this part of *Liber Novus* Jung goes through a metaphorical process of psychiatric internment as he is apparently alienated from reality. He is removed to a psychiatric hospital and is taken through the procedures associated with an emergency internment. This part of the book is a criticism of the ritual of internment and the classic psychiatric interrogation. Jung is interviewed by the head doctor, who assumes a typically authoritarian attitude.

Professor: "What's that book you've got there?"

[Jung]:   "It's Thomas à Kempis, *The Imitation of Christ*."

Professor: "So, a form of religious madness, perfectly clear, religious paranoia.—You see, my dear, nowadays the imitation of Christ leads to the madhouse."

[Jung]:   "That is hardly to be doubted, professor."

Professor: "The man has wit—he is obviously somewhat maniacally aroused. Do you hear voices? … Are the voices following you?"

[Jung]: "Oh no, Heaven forbid, I summon them."

Professor: "Ah, this is yet another case that clearly indicates that hallucination directly calls up voices. This belongs in the case history. Would you immediately make a note of that, doctor?"

[Jung]: "With all due respect, professor, may I say that it is absolutely not abnormal, but much rather the intuitive method."

Professor: "Excellent. The fellow also uses neologisms. Well—I suppose we have an adequately clear diagnosis. Anyway, I wish you a good recovery, and make sure you stay quiet."

[Jung]: "But professor, I am not at all sick, I feel perfectly well."

Professor: "Look, my dear. You don't have any insight into your illness yet. The prognosis is naturally pretty bad, with at best limited recovery." (p. 295)

In this classic psychiatric interview, which may differ a little or perhaps not at all from the psychiatric interviews carried out in present-day first consultations, various opportunities to develop a deeper understanding of the patient are ignored and reduced to symptoms and psychopathological defences. The book by Thomas à Kempis is interpreted as a form of religious madness or religious paranoia. A possible sense of humour leads to the patient being described as maniacally aroused. The classic *auditory phonemes* are used to confirm a psychopathological diagnosis, without delving any deeper into the evaluation of the patient. When the patient himself demonstrates superior intellectual sophistication, saying that he feels perfectly well, and that the conversations he has with the images are the result of an intuitive method, this is then classified in the psychiatric evaluation as a typical symptom of a psychotic crisis, in this case the formation of a new language or the use of neologisms. Jung then passes through an experience in a psychiatric hospital, where he is interned in a ward with other patients.

Jung uses this humorous (and at the same time tragic) metaphor of a psychiatric internment to make a damning criticism of the medical model of the time that was devoid of any symbolic perspective. At the same time, developing this metaphor further he shows that he is conscious that with *Liber Novus* he is proposing a method of dialogue with the unconscious that is so new and revolutionary that it could easily be confused with madness, and possession by the unconscious and its images. This matter and the boundaries between conscious logic and the apparent irrationality of the unconscious and its challenges will be discussed in the final chapter.

The legend of the Holy Grail guides the way

On the third level of this symbolic experience we find the legend of the Holy Grail. Jung sees elements of the Arthurian saga parade before him on a stage. First there is the hero Parsifal, with whom he identifies. In this representation, the legend of the Holy Grail acquires a significant importance. Historically and symbolically, the Arthurian circle represents the creative bringing together of elements from European paganism and Christianity. In this fantasy, the myth represents a way out for the cultural dissociation of the West. As discussed previously, Jung had already presented images of madness that were different to the vision of the time and relativised the rigidity of Western psychiatric nosology. At other points in his work, Jung provides examples of mythology from Ancient Greece, aboriginal, and medieval European storytelling traditions and the customs of tribal societies in order to propose creative approaches to the limits between normality and madness.

The legend of the Holy Grail is highly complex, and there are various versions and variations. It has been discussed by a range of Jungian authors, the most well known of these being Emma Jung and Von Franz (Jung, E. & Von Franz, 1989; Von Franz, 1975 and Cardoso, 1995). The legend has a substantial amount of symbolic content, as it brings together pre-Christian and Christian elements, and is an important symbol of the process of individuation as described by Jung. Historically, the legend of the Holy Grail forms a link between paganism and Christianity, as pagan elements are inserted in a fundamentally Christian theme. The elements of the legend that appear in *Liber Novus* are associated with the version that Wagner used for his opera *Parsifal*. Shamdasani comments on these essential elements in one of his footnotes:

> Titurel and his Christian knights have the Holy Grail in their keeping in their castle, with a sacred spear to guard it. Klingsor is a sorcerer who seeks the Grail. He has enticed the keepers of the Grail into his magic garden, where there are flower maidens and the enchantress Kundry. Amfortas, Titurel's son, goes into the castle

to destroy Klingsor but is enchanted by Kundry and lets the sacred spear fall, and Klingsor wounds him with it.

Amfortas needs the touch of the spear to heal his wound … A voice from the Grail sanctuary prophesises that only a youth who is guileless and innocent can regain the spear. Parsifal … not knowing his name or the name of his father, the knights hope that he is this youth. Klingsor orders Kundry to seduce Parsifal. Parsifal defeats Klingsor's knights. Kundry is transformed into a beautiful woman, and she kisses him. From this, he realises that Kundry seduced Amfortas, and he resists her. Klingsor hurls the spear at him, and Parsifal seizes it.

Klingsor's castle and garden disappear … Parsifal baptises Kundry. They go into the castle and ask Amfortas to uncover the Grail. Amfortas asks them to slay him. Parsifal enters and touches his wound with the spear. Amfortas is transfigured, and Parsifal radiantly holds up the Grail. (p. 303)

After leaving behind the mysterious cook and his incubation experience, Jung enters a stage, where the myth of the Holy Grail is being re-enacted. First he sees the hero Parsifal wearing black armour, and he is shocked to discover that Amfortas and the damsel Kundry look almost identical to the librarian and the cook.

Jung describes his strange experience with the Grail as follows:

I saw a high-ceilinged hall before me—with a supposedly magnificent garden in the background, Klingsor's magical garden, it occurred to me at once. I had entered a theatre: those two there are part of the play:

Amfortas and Kundry; or rather, just what am I looking at? It is the librarian and his cook. He is ailing and pale, and has a bad stomach, she is disappointed and furious. Klingsor is standing to the left, holding the feather used to tuck behind his ear.

How closely Klingsor resembles me! What a repulsive play! But look, Parsifal enters from the left. How strange, he also looks like me. Klingsor venomously throws the feather at Parsifal. But the latter catches it calmly.

The scene changes: it appears that the audience, in this case me, joins in during the last act. One must kneel down as the Good Friday service begins: Parsifal enters (…) Parsifal takes off his helmet.

Kundry stands in the distance, covering her head and laughing. The audience is enraptured and recognises itself in Parsifal. He is I. I take off my armour layered with history and my chimerical decoration and go to the spring wearing a white penitent's shirt, where I wash my feet and hands without the help of a stranger. Then also take off my penitent's shirt and put on my civilian clothes. I walk out of the scene and approach myself, I who am still kneeling down in prayer as the audience. I rise and become one with myself. (pp. 302–303)

The mysterious familiarity between the different characters of this mythical drama and previous figures in Jung's experience points to the fact that they are related and provide explanation for one another. Amfortas the wounded king is the expression in the Western cultural unconscious of dissociated rationality; this dissociation is also represented by the figure of the librarian. Trying to counter the threat presented by the sorcerer Klingsor, Amfortas becomes victim to Kundry, the damsel sent by Klingsor. Kundry belongs to the group of damsels linked to Klingsor's garden. Her name means "the message carrier", from the German *Kunde*, which means "news" or "information" (Derrick, 2011), a characteristic that is attributed to the damsels in the magic garden. This means that she is an *anima* figure, the great bringer of enigmas. The presence of the magical garden is a reference to a paradise free of opposites. The symbol of the garden can be found in a great many myths and artistic representations. Firstly, it is the garden of the first couple in the Bible, the Garden of Eden. From a Judaeo-Christian point of view, the garden represents integration with nature, which also belongs to the unconscious. The expulsion from Eden, in this respect, represents the beginning of individual consciousness and free will. From a psychological point of view, the serpent here acquires the role of the *anima,* and is the bringer of the conscious.[4]

Gardens were always seen as sacred in Ancient Greece and represented the union of nature and culture, an important integration of the natural and civilised worlds. The goddess Aphrodite was the lady of gardens and the goddess Flora, her hypostasis, was the guardian of flowers (see also Paris, 1986). There is also the Garden of Hesperides, where Aphrodite's golden apples are kept, and the Garden of Delights depicted in the painting by Hieronymus Bosch with its surprising symbolism, among others. The garden, full of seduction, belongs to the sorcerer Klingsor, who is an important symbol of the regressive libido, the energy that leads to the primordial state of fusion and away from differentiation.

Kundry is able to seduce Amfortas and make him unable to confront Klingsor, who wounds him using the magical spear that Amfortas himself had let fall. Jung describes this as being similar to the librarian's feather. The weapon of reason is unable on its own to decipher the enigma of the unconscious presented by Kundry the anima. This theme reappears in the play *Oedipus Rex*, where the hero confronts another typical figure of the anima, the Sphinx, which also provides an enigma to be solved.[5]

Oedipus follows the classic model of the omnipotent hero and tries to solve the enigma in a purely rational way: "It is man". The Sphinx plunges into the abyss and the hero enters triumphantly into the city. We already know his tragic destiny, however, and that the regressive anima will triumph in the end. In a similar way, Amfortas cannot establish an adequate relationship with the mysterious anima Kundry using the weapons of reason, is seduced by her, falls into Klingsor's power, and becomes the Wounded King, or Fisher King, removed of his royal power.

This passage about the wounding of Amfortas is an example of the profound myth of the wounded healer. The magic spear that Amfortas drops is the same spear that Klingsor uses magically to petrify him. Could this be the same spear that the Roman centurion uses to pierce the side of the King of the Jews? Amfortas is also a king, and symbolically the king is a model of good behaviour, the ego ideal for any culture, and the model that everybody should resemble. While Christ as King of the Jews is a symbol of the self in Western culture, the king Amfortas represents Western man and his rational dissociation, who is incapable of forming a relationship between the world of conscious reasoning and the symbolic world of the unconscious. The same spear that wounds and disassociates must be used in the correct way to cure and transform.

The figure of Parsifal, who does not know his own name or the name of his father, represents consciousness emptied of old family and cultural values. The hero of the Holy Grail has this type of consciousness as the new wine of spiritual renovation must be put into new wineskins.

Only he has his ears pricked and hears Kundry's message, who in the role of the messenger archetype tells him his father's real name, preparing him for his spiritual rebirth.

The return to the magical garden of childhood is the desire that runs through every neurosis. Jung formulated a way out of the garden within the primordial polarisation of the ego-unconscious or mother-baby duality through the interference of a third person, a *tertio quid non datur*. This is represented either by the concrete figure of the father or by an inner ability the child develops by internalising the regulating principle of what is right or wrong and the cultural prohibitions necessary for a healthy development. The tertiary structure is fundamental in the organisation of the personality. Jung developed the theory of the creation of this third space, which is where the self manifests in the development of the personality, in his essay "The Transcendent Function", written around the same time as *The Red Book*.

The legend of the Holy Grail, with its Celtic elements revitalising Christian symbols, the Grail, the Fisher King and the Wounded King, among others, appears in *Liber Novus* as a possible way to overcome the one-sidedness of modern life. Jung had recently written his work *Symbols of Transformation*, in which he uncovers the true redeeming role of the myth in modern day life. Myths represent a bridge between the rational mind and the apparent irrational language of the unconscious, and are the key to overcoming disassociations. According to Jung, disassociations are the central element of the neuroses and of all psychic suffering. The theatrical representation of the legend of the Holy Grail seems to try to demonstrate these possibilities. After discovering the importance of myths for our culture, Jung embarked on another project: to discover his personal myth. This was the start of *The Red Book*.[6]

CHAPTER SIX

New perspectives in Jungian clinical practice

> "The individual is a gateway … the issue is not simply solving individual neuroses, individual suffering, but dealing with those aspects where the individual suffering intersects, coheres, is in direct connection with collective problems"
> —Sonu Shamdasani (Hillman & Shamdasani, 2013, p. 151)

James Hillman dedicates the chapter "The Pandemonium of Images" of his book *Healing Fiction* (1983) to the Jungian method of psychotherapy. The name of this chapter summarises the Jungian method, a constant confrontation with figures of the unconscious, a powerful technique based on the method of active imagination that Jung developed while writing *Liber Novus*. Hillman mentions (p. 53) that "Jung gave a distinct response to our culture's most persistent psychological need—from Oedipus to Socrates through Hamlet and Faust—Know Thyself."

In fact, the major emphasis of *The Red Book* is the role played by its characters in Jung's personal myth and their meaning in his individuation process. However, the book also presents new perspectives for a revolutionary type of clinical practice. *Liber Novus* in its entirety can be seen as a sort of self-analysis by the author, who is searching for understanding during a time of significant transition, in which *he is the patient, the method, and also his own analyst.*

The transcendent function and active imagination

The theory of some central aspects of clinical practice was developed by Jung in his text *The Transcendent Function*, a revolutionary essay that is now considered to be one of his most fundamental pieces of work. Written in 1917, around the same time as *The Red Book*, it was highly influenced by Jung's experiences at the time. The essay has such a striking character that the author was reluctant to publish it, as he was concerned that it would be misunderstood. The fate of this essay was similar to that of *The Red Book*, which was kept out of the public realm until some students of the C. G. Jung Institute in Zurich discovered it by accident in 1958, leading to its publication.

I believe that *The Transcendent Function* has an enormous importance among Jung's *Collected Works*, as it discusses the spontaneous production of symbols by the unconscious coherently and in a way that is theoretically valid. *The Transcendent Function* is in no way related to the four functions that Jung later developed in his work on the psychological types. It is related to the spontaneous production of a third element out of the tension of opposing factors, which maintains both conscious and unconscious value. This third element, which he named a *Tertium quid non datur* (from the Latin "A third possibility that can not be classified according to two previous possibilities"), is the symbolic image that indicates a creative way out from the tension of opposites inherent to psychological conflict. Some saw in these complex ideas an important influence by the philosopher Friedrich Hegel, whose philosophical proposal on the dynamics of history was based on the opposition between a thesis and an antithesis leading to a synthesis. This new synthesis would then act as a new thesis on a higher level, and so on.[1]

The production of symbols by the unconscious demonstrates the creativity of the self and the ability of the central archetype to construct new pathways. This symbolism is independent of conscious will and reveals the organising function of the self. This theory that defines a creative aspect in the unconscious through the production of symbols was completely revolutionary.

Freud once commented that there were three great wounds to humanity's narcissism (1916–1917). The first was Copernicus's theory of heliocentricity, demonstrating that the Earth was not the centre of the universe, the second was Darwin's theory of evolution, showing that man was not directly created in the image of God but evolved from the higher anthropoids, and the third was the theory of psychoanalysis, which revealed that man was not in control of his own behaviour. Although this claim may be true, as his systematic exploration of the unconscious was indeed revolutionary, he always described the id—his new structure within the unconscious—as a completely disorganised bundle of drives without direction. The psyche would be organised by the ego, which is essential so that the individual can live a healthy and balanced life. "Where id was, there shall ego be" was his motto for psychological progress.

Jung had to demonstrate the presence of the centre of totality, with its conscious and unconscious processes, representing the self with its capacity to organise the totality of the psyche and give direction to the process of individuation through symbolic production. This was Jung's fundamental contribution to the findings of psychoanalysis. He demonstrated this symbolic activity of the self through the transcendent function with his systematic study of a series of dreams and fantasies. These images will always point the way and will always have a purpose and *end* that is completely removed from the subject's consciousness.[2] The transcendent function manifests through vivid symbols that indicate new pathways. These symbols of objects, characters, animals, and situations should be approached as though they have an objective reality. This is a fundamental process in the psychological transformation of the dreamer. This intense imaginative process during the writing of *Liber Novus* was the start of Jung's active imagination technique. *The Red Book* itself can be seen as a continuous process of active imagination, as it involves a dialectic confrontation with a large variety of internal characters and a polyphony of subjective dialogues. Jung's basic postulate is at work here: autonomous emotions have a lot of power over the ego, possessing it and exerting a lot of dissociative power over the conscious. When these emotions are personified, the conscious can enter into dialogue with them, and it is through this dialectic posture that content can be better integrated. This is the essence of the therapeutic value of psychological personification, one of the central postulates of analytic psychology and an essential element in *Liber Novus*. The personification of psychic content can be found throughout the book, which encourages the integration of energy previously belonging to the unconscious. There is a gradual personification of the so-called *Spirit of the Depths*, for example, which initially manifests as an impersonal voice, then as Elijah, a wise prophet from the Old Testament, and later on as the central guide of the book, the wise Gnostic character Philemon, who personifies the *wise old man archetype*, the principle of reflection and the guide of the conscious (the gradual personification of the archetype of this spirit in *Liber Novus* is discussed in more detail in Chapter Nine). As these personifications occur, the ego's dialogues with them become more intense and an appropriation of the energy of this content becomes possible (this is not an *identification*, which is radically different). This ultimately leads to a transformation of the conscious personality.

Carefully observing the statements made in *The Transcendent Function* (Jung, 1958), it is possible to see suggestions of therapeutic approaches based entirely on the author's personal experience. When Jung mentions that the transcendent function is the psychological function that brings together conceptual aspects and the aesthetic of the psyche, he affirms something that I consider to be central to psychotherapy. This essential discovery is the theoretic basis for the great value that expressive techniques have gained in Jungian therapy.

Through this important insight that psychic life unfolds into two fundamental aspects—one conceptual and the other aesthetic—Jung opens up the opportunity for reflection on a matter that has huge clinical importance. Indeed, the psychological symbol is predominantly aesthetic, as it comes to us in the form of an image, and it has a conceptual core with a polysemy of meanings. When in *Liber Novus* the author makes use of aesthetic, imagistic language through its characters, symbols, experiences, and various expressions to expand on a series of theoretical concepts, he is establishing a therapeutic approach in which the aesthetic category of representation has an important role.

The four verbs

The confrontation with inner images takes place according to the four verbs, or stages, according to Jung:

1. *Empty*—The mind is emptied of its everyday content so that new images can appear spontaneously from the unconscious.

2. *Let go*—The conscious suspends its interference of arising images and they follow their own course. They are free and present their own discourse, independent of the conscious mind.
3. *Impregnate*—Provided with adequate psychological space, images grow, acquire density, and take up a significant presence in the conscious mind.
4. *Confront ethically*—Only now can the conscious mind act, taking an ethical position in relation to the unconscious "other". This final step is necessary and essential, as otherwise states of possession or identification with internal images can occur.[3]

This process of confrontation with internal images was an essential process in the creation of *The Red Book*, and Jung named it active imagination.

Possibilities of symbolic integration

Discussing the relationships between individuals and their unconscious images during the process of active imagination, Jung also distinguished four distinct types of people. The visual type, the auditory type that can "hear" their inner voices, those who express unconscious material with their hands, and the rarest category, the motor-sensory type, who are able to express their unconscious through the movements of their body and dance. An unusual process used to access the unconscious is also cited, called automatic writing, where notes are written directly onto a clipboard.

There is a wide range of creative possibilities available to confront the unconscious, which are being developed in various ways by many different schools of modern therapy. These different ways of circling psychic images, gradually integrating and processing them on every individual's personal journey make up a wide and varied model of therapy that was revolutionary for the age in which it arose (1917).

Let us explore each of these possibilities in more detail. Firstly, for the visual type it is vital that the image, its intrinsic mystery, and its element of the unknown are respected, as it originates from the "other" of the collective unconscious. The representation that spontaneously emerges from the unconscious must be respected in its original form, regardless of conscious will. Individuals who are highly visual should wait for the image to form in their mind and note how it appears without interpreting it. Concepts formed by the ego at this time will only inhibit the spontaneous manifestation of this personal material.

With the auditory type, which is much less common than the former, the unconscious manifests through a voice, phrase, or a seemingly irrational command. Jung recalls the familiar voices that are frequently observed in serious mental disorders, known as *phonemes*, considered by traditional psychiatry to be typical of psychosis (1958). The fundamental difference between psychosis and the creative confrontation with the unconscious is the presence or not of literalisation, which is the way in which a mentally ill individual believes the voice to be real and responds to it as a command that must be obeyed at any price. When assumed to be purely symbolic, the voice is seen as a symbol and the content of what is being said as something unfamiliar and complex that cannot be immediately understood. The symbolic content of the message is seen from the beginning as a mystery to be gradually solved.

Jung had an auditory experience while he was writing his second *Black Book*. Recording his experiences, Jung reports having clearly heard the voice of a woman saying, "What you do is not science, it is art," Jung told how he became intensely worried with what the voice had said. He wanted to maintain the scientific integrity of his method at any cost, and in the end he found an intuitive response to what the voice had said, answering, "No, what I do is nature" (1963, p. 178).

Jung's active imagination demonstrates a way in which relating to unconscious material is taken seriously. The challenging female voice represents his inner need to create a new method that will bring together conceptual (science) and aesthetic (artistic) elements. The creative insight that Jung had with his concept of the *transcendent function* is his way of bringing these two aspects together. The art–science opposition is valid just for the natural sciences, biology, physics, and chemistry. Analytic psychology and psychoanalysis are not sciences, despite repeated affirmations from Freud and Jung that they are. These are the *knowledge* of a newly emerging paradigm. Strictly speaking, the sciences include everything that can be tested in a laboratory and that is subject to repetition, hypothesis, and prognosis. Freud's and Jung's depth psychology, which works with the unconscious, cannot be included in this category. The art–science dichotomy has been relativised by Thomas Khun's notion of the transition of paradigms (1962). In the same way, the whole of *Liber Novus* reconciles both the conceptual and aesthetic aspects of the psyche.

Individuals capable of artistic expression are more common than may be expected. Perhaps as a result of cultural influences or family pressure, people often tend to abandon their genuine artistic capabilities. Jung held this form of personal expression in high esteem, perhaps because since his own childhood his hands had had a fundamental role in the expression of his fantasies. It is true that this happens to a certain extent with all children, as they play in a more physical and artistic way than adults do. Artists are an important exception to this rule and bring their contact with the polymorphous creative child into their adult lives.[4] Children express their fantasies with their hands through *bricolage*, a huge range of seemingly endless drawings and games.[5] The games that Jung played as a child, his small toy that he sculpted into his school case and with whom he would talk in his childhood fantasies, seem to have carried through into his sculptures, drawings, and paintings as an adult. During his stay in Paris in 1901 and 1902, Jung tried his hand at being a painter, creating a range of rather expressive landscapes. (These paintings can be seen in Jaffé, 1979.) The paintings in *Liber Novus* demonstrate this continuous integration between the verbal and the non-verbal. It is therefore not surprising that Jung sought to add an *aesthetic emphasis* to his therapeutic approach. Without a doubt, he was one of the great pioneers of non-verbal strategies in psychotherapy.

Emphasising the pioneering role that Jung had in naturally expressed therapeutic strategies does not mean that he was the only one to have developed these. Others have made a decisive contribution to the development of an aesthetic perspective in therapy, such as the therapeutic artist Margareth Naumburg and the psychoanalyst Ernst Kris, among others. The Swiss Jungian psychoanalyst Dora Kalff was an important proponent of the aesthetic method in therapy with her sand tray technique.[6] In Brazil, Nise da Silveira (1980) made an original and important contribution using the aesthetic method with psychotic patients in large hospitals. These are just some examples of non-verbal techniques that are widely used by a range of Jungian therapists.

Among the non-verbal methods, the motor-sensory type of active imagination has been explored further in more recent times. Gesture and movement are ways of expressing inner processes. Chodorow (1986) mentions the fact that on at least one known occasion, Jung used this method of active imagination using expressive movement. He encouraged one of his patients, who had started to draw a mandala, to finish it through the medium of dance. The use of movement in Jungian therapy is well known. After graduating in dance, Mary Whitehouse studied at the C. G. Jung Institute in Zurich and qualified as a Jungian analyst. She then sought to integrate expressive movement into Jungian analysis and created a therapeutic approach called "authentic movement". Joan Chodorow and Janet Adler were both important figures in the development of the School of Authentic Movement. This therapy uses a type of active imagination in which unconscious content is expressed directly through movement. The body and its gestures are the spontaneous means through which symbols manifest in therapy (Chodorow, 1986, 2008).

Jung's proposals for a new type of psychotherapy in *The Red Book* are more in the area of active imagination and the expressive techniques. This is the process that was referred to as the *non-talking cure* in Chapter Four (in contrast to Anna O.'s *talking cure*). These creative pathways free up analysis from the classic approach, which although useful in some cases, is losing ground to creative solutions that are less rigid, but at the same time still consistent. These approaches are more appropriate for the modern individual who lives in a fast-paced life and has more urgent demands. Financial issues, lack of time, and multiple forms of communication through the internet have overtaken the more rigid models of five consultations per week on the couch.

Transference and active imagination

The process described by Freud that he called *transference* (from the German *Übertragung*, meaning to transport or to take from one place to another) is the phenomenon by which elements from childhood, expectations, and varied experiences are projected onto the analyst. The therapeutic setting acts as a way of repeating past situations that have been repressed in the unconscious. This basic process is very important and central to any therapeutic experience. The patient unwittingly re-edits the issues retained in his unconscious, which enables him to resolve these through careful interpretation-based analysis.

Jungian analysis has its own understanding of transference, in which it contains personal aspects of unintegrated childhood experiences but is also an important vehicle for archetypical experiences from the collective unconscious as part of the individuation process. In addition, although transference and countertransference processes have always received a lot of attention in therapy, it should not be forgotten that human relations processes also occur *pari passu*. The client and therapist are both present as individuals, each with his own values, memories, and preferences. It is important to recognise that these processes exist without allowing the analytic process to be compromised. Jung emphasised that if the analyst does not like at least one aspect of his client, he is incapable of treating him. The Jungian analyst Mario Jacoby expanded on these issues in his book *The Analytic Encounter* (1984).

Liber Novus is the basis for all of Jung's theoretic constructions on the individuation process and its fundamental stages. The various characters that emerge in the imaginary encounters in the book led Jung to systemise a process for the development of the personality based on a dialectic with inner figures that he named the *persona*, the *shadow*, the *anima*, the *animus*, the *mana-personality*, and the *self*. These stages were theoretically elaborated at the end of the period of the confrontation with the unconscious in the essay *The Relations between the Ego and the Unconscious* (Jung, 1928). The various characters representing specific moments of this process also appear in an individual's transference, lending it more colour. The therapeutic setting can therefore be seen as a therapeutic vase containing the images of transformation that are part of the psychological process, where each patient writes his own *Red Book*.

Let us cite a clinical example in order to better understand how an archetypical configuration can appear as part of the transference.[7] I once received a call from somebody who had been referred to me by a friend; she had not had any previous contact with me. As I did not have time to see her immediately, she had to wait a week for her first consultation. During this wait, she had a dream that she told me about at the beginning of her analysis:

> I was in an unfamiliar open field. I discovered a slope and went down it into a wide cave. Spurred on by my curiosity, I started to explore the inside of the cavern, which went on and on like a huge labyrinth. In the middle of this huge labyrinth there was an old bald man surrounded by a group of people. I thought, 'It's my analyst,' and I waited for my turn to be seen.

This is the type of dream that Jung named the *initial dream*, which would turn out to have an interesting meaning for the whole process that was to follow. This prophetic aspect is perhaps due to the fact that this is the first therapeutic setting in which projections and resistance can take place on both sides (those of both the client and the analyst, as the latter also has his own transference and unconscious resistance towards the patient). In these conditions, the unconscious appears clearly and some of the anticipatory aspects of its symbols can be felt. The unconscious is timeless and in certain situations can present anticipatory aspects of the therapeutic process.

This dream contains archetypal aspects: the grotto in the form of a labyrinth (an element present in old initiations and a symbol of the unconscious) and the important symbol of the *wise old man* archetype. The analyst appears as the wise old man, surrounded by his followers or patients, and the client must patiently wait her turn. This is an example of transference of idealisation, as the analyst (who at the time is completely unknown to the patient) appears surrounded by *mana* ("a mysterious force") and power. This strong transference of idealisation has both positive and negative effects on the process. It is positive as it shows the patient's emotional investment, and her desire to explore the labyrinth (her own unconscious) reveals her openness and interest in the analytic process. It also shows the extent to which she trusts the analyst and the process that she is about to start. However, the analyst taking on the role of the wise old man who holds all the power for cure and transformation is a negative aspect. This projection of an archetypal image leads to problems associated with the omnipotence of the analyst (who feels he is the master of cure and is attributed magical powers by his patients) and the infantilisation of the patient, who becomes highly dependent on her (or his) analyst. These turn into the so-called *interminable analyses* in which the patient is incapable of getting in touch with the image of the wise old man within herself. This is because the wise old man archetype belongs to the collective unconscious and not exclusively to the analyst. It is an unconscious aspect of the patient herself that she needs to recover. Indeed, it represents the power of reflection (from the Latin *reflectere*, meaning "to turn backwards") and the ability to discover creative ways out of existential problems.

The mythological and archetypal themes of this transferential fantasy can also be observed in Jung's fantasies during the writing of *Liber Novus*: the theme of descent (in the chapter "Descent into Hell in the Future" in *Liber Primus*) and the encounter with the wise old man archetype (Elijah and later Philemon). These fantasies brought about the theoretical construct of the individuation process that reappears in therapy in the symbolic material expressed and in the transference.

I have also observed the frequent appearance of the wise old man archetype at the start of the process in dreams and transferential fantasies. In another clinical example, a patient had an initial dream in which she saw herself walking through the neighbourhood of Ipanema in Rio de Janeiro, when she saw an old man watching her from a window of a building. He looked wise and a little like her grandfather, who was a dominant personality in the family and was much loved and respected. At the same time, the old man vaguely reminded her of me. In this example, there are elements of transference present. Why does this image of the wise old man appear so often at the beginning of therapy? Shouldn't this archetype, which is intimately linked to the self, be dominant during the later phases of analysis? My hypothesis is that patients seeking therapy are immersed in a *compulsion to repetition*, as Freud called it, which is the essence of neurosis. They are passing through a time of reflection, thinking about their lives and their need to seek help and change. At this time the patient is under the unconscious influence of the wise old man archetype, or the principle of reflection. This is why he frequently manifests in dreams and fantasies.

Another aspect of this archetype (and this is valid for all archetypes) is that he isn't situated in the transcendental realm outside everyday experience. In the majority of families there are striking figures that organise the family group and who serve as an example, are admired and revered. This is generally a grandfather or grandmother figure who leaves a significant mark in the history of the family. When such a person dies, the absence of the *numinous*, catalysing force of the wise old man or wise old woman is strongly felt. The structure of the family disintegrates and divorce and other radical changes start to take place. The cohesion of the group as a whole is threatened as the integrating power of the symbol is no longer an influence on the family unconscious.

The clinical pathway and the symbolic pathway

These clinical examples reveal an important element: the union and interdependence of the analysis of the transference and the analysis of archetypal figures. In the past there was a false dichotomy between the symbolic method and the clinical method, leading to the opinion that Jungian analysts interpreted dreams and symbols while Freudian analysts were more interested in transference. This interpretation is incorrect and already seen as outdated. The symbolic and the clinical can exist side by side, with the archetypal figures of the individuation process existing within the clinical context.

Jung's personal experience while he was writing *Liber Novus* led him to develop a profoundly personal approach to the therapeutic process that avoided formulas, rigid theories, and general rules applicable to all cases. This personal perspective had already led Jung to suggest to Freud that didactic analysis should be mandatory for all students of psychoanalysis, and that only those who have confronted their own unconscious are fit to be analysts. He also emphasised that the analyst can only take the analysand to where he has previously been! This statement was far from the classic vision of the distant analyst, who was not involved in the *opus* of their client. Each analysis is a new challenge. There is no monotony in the interpretation, as general theories have just relative value. With the intense experience of his own unconscious that he expressed in *The Red Book*, Jung invites us to write our own *Red Book* and confront our own images.

CHAPTER SEVEN

The legacy of the dead

"These figures are the dead, not just your dead, that is, all the images of the shapes you took in the past, which your ongoing life has left behind, but also the thronging dead of human history, the ghostly procession of the past, which is an ocean compared to the drops of your own life span"

—*Liber Secundus*, "Nox Secunda"

"Immortal mortals, mortal immortals, one living the others' death and dying the others' life"

—Heraclitus of Ephesus, "The Obscure", Fragment 62 (Bornheim, 2002)

The dead appear in a range of forms at various moments in *The Red Book*, always as part of an imaginary dialogue with Jung. In one example, the soul of a woman is anxiously seeking a talisman that will answer her questions. She reminds Jung of one of his former patients who had passed away. There are other examples, such as in the intriguing Chapter 13 of *Liber Secundus*, "The Sacrificial Murder", in which Jung discovers a dead child and speaks with its soul, giving him a nearly impossible task to complete. Another important confrontation with the dead takes place in Chapter 15 of *Liber Secundus*, "Nox Secunda", discussed in Chapter Five. After the librarian gives him *The Imitation of Christ* by the Benedictine monk Thomas à Kempis, Jung waits in the anteroom of the library. He hears the sound of voices and shadowy figures pass by. One of these looks at him with tired eyes. This man reveals his name, Ezechiel, declaring that he is an Anabaptist,[1] leaving together with the throngs around him to seek truths and revelations in Jerusalem. Jung shows an interest in following him to seek these truths, but Ezechiel responds that he cannot, as he still has a body. He then declares, "We are the dead" (p. 294).

Of all the apparitions and interferences of the dead in *The Red Book*, the most important takes place in the third part, *Scrutinies*, when Philemon gives the Seven Sermons to the Dead (*Septem Sermones ad Mortuos*). The hordes of the dead coming from Jerusalem "did not find what they were seeking", as though they were indoctrinated by Philemon on the nature of God, man, and destiny. The hordes of the dead appeared during Jung's confrontation with the unconscious through a series of psychological phenomena that took place at his house (1963, p. 182). This chapter discusses the possible reasons for this intense presence of the dead in *The Red Book* and the role that these had in the life and works of Jung.

Ancestor worship and the origins of religion

The dead have always been surrounded by extremely rigorous taboos and rituals. The purpose of these rituals was to separate the realm of the living from the realm of the dead through effective symbols. Propitiatory rituals still exist in contemporary culture through a range of ceremonies, such as the mass of the seventh day in Catholicism and the Matzeiva in Judaism. Judaism also has a traditional custom of covering mirrors for a certain time to stop the dead from staying attached to their image and remaining among the living.

There are many rituals associated with the cult of the dead that are specific to communities in Brazil. In Santa Rosa and various small communities in the states of Rio Grande do Sul and Paraná, there is an unusual ritual called the "covering of the soul". When somebody dies, a piece of their clothing is given to a person considered to be of good character so that their soul is well dressed when they enter heaven. This is because the clothes of the dead stay with him in the tomb, and he needs some others to get into heaven. The person that uses these clothes becomes close to the family and almost a representative of the deceased. In the case of children, they become a godson to the family.[2]

Since the beginnings of civilisation, the fear of the dead returning, known as *revenants* (meaning "those who return"), has been the basis for a wide range of propitiatory rituals. In anthropology and religious studies these rituals are considered to be the origin of religion itself and the belief in life after death has existed since early periods of cultural existence. (See also Eliade, 1983.) The first rituals can be seen on Neanderthal tombs, in which the dead were buried in the foetal position to enable their rebirth in another life. Animal sacrifices in these tombs also seem to indicate that religion and mythology came about as a result of a cult of the dead (Armstrong, 2005). If these rituals ward off the fear of invasion by unknown spirits, they also reveal veneration and religious respect and the notion that the dead are of value and protect the living. In Ancient Greece, ancestor worship was the origin of the hero cult, the protecting hero actually being a deified person from the past who had died and become an entity that protected the city. (See also Brandão, 1987.)

Possible symbolic interpretations of the dead

The dead are an important key to the understanding of *Liber Novus*, and perhaps one of the most important. There is a prevailing idea that they need to be saved and that something must be done to integrate this energy within the collective unconscious that manifests in the form of those who have died.

> The number of the unredeemed dead has become greater that the number of living Christians; therefore it is time that we accept the dead. (p. 297)

The encounter with a group of the dead, murmuring like "a frenzied flapping of wings" is repeated in the third part of the book, *Scrutinies*, when Philemon gives the enigmatic Seven Sermons to the Dead. This moment is the climax of *Liber Novus*. It involves a process of indoctrination and recovery. Ezechiel the Anabaptist previously declared that he and the hordes of the dead were going to Jerusalem to visit the most sacred of tombs, and now the dead returning from Jerusalem declare that they did not find what they were seeking. At the beginning of the sermons, an agitated and murmuring throng of the dead approaches Jung. The seven sermons are proffered to them, and they question Philemon, who in turn responds in Gnostic parables. After each sermon, the dead become either more agitated or calmer, reacting in a different way to each sermon. It seems that the intention of Philemon's speech is to satisfy the dead in their search for knowledge of the mysteries of life, God, man, and his destiny. This really is a profound mystery. What is the meaning of this near omnipresence of the dead in *The Red Book*?

One explanation that has been given for this is that we ourselves are the dead who cannot find the answers in established religion and need something new and experiential, or Gnostic (to be obtained through *gnosis*, or knowledge), a vivid new truth (consistent with the name *Liber Novus*!) that makes sense to our souls and that has not suffered the wear of automatic convention.[3] The old classic truths from Jerusalem (the Judaeo-Christian myth) worn down by the millennia are no longer satisfactory.

The symbolic interpretation that Jung gives for the dead is that they generally represent something in us that has not been redeemed and returns in search of a way forward, an answer or redemption. The dead are contents from the psychological shadow that come back in order to be integrated into the conscious. These are abandoned parts of the psyche that have been forgotten and that lie dormant in the past, typical of unwanted or repressed content (Jung, 1963, p. 278).

Another approach has a historical premise. *Liber Novus* was written at the time of the First World War, the great European crisis in which hundreds of thousands of young men were sent to their deaths on the battlefield. The unimaginable number of dead across the whole of Europe invaded the collective imagination. The cruelty of death and the destiny of the dead were issues that were present in the minds of everybody, including Jung.[4]

The dead in the life and work of Jung

All these approaches are convincing to a certain extent. However, are they sufficiently comprehensive? We cannot forget that the dead were of particular interest to Jung from a very early age, according to what he wrote in *Memories, Dreams, Reflections*. One of Jung's first memories was from when he was around four years old, when he was at home and heard a commotion. A body had been found in the Rhine. The body was placed at the back of the house in the laundry. Jung was taken over by an irresistible curiosity often found in children and snuck through a window at the back of the house to get a secret glimpse of the body. The trickle of blood on the floor filled him with curiosity (p. 22).

It seems that death was an important issue for Jung long before he wrote *Liber Novus*, meaning that the dead were part of his personal myth and his individuation process. It is known that Jung's family on his mother's side had a close relationship with spiritual manifestations. Samuel Preiswerk, Jung's maternal grandfather, had visions of the dead that interfered in the preparation of his sermons as a pastor. Jung's cousin on his mother's side held seances, which he studied for his doctorate thesis in medicine. The various spirits that manifested themselves through Helène Preiswerk were deconstructed by Jung as psychological fragments, a clear demonstration of the capacity of the psyche to spontaneously disassociate.[5]

Jung's research into these phenomena was rigorously empirical, and he used his findings in his doctorate thesis while he was studying at the University of Basel. His concepts of the disassociability of the psyche and the autonomy of psychic fragments were developed in these studies and became fundamental in the later formulation of his complex theory. These so-called *spirits of the dead* were seen here as psychic autonomous complexes, fragments of the psyche that had not been integrated into the conscious. There is also the idea that these psychological fragments can be personified. Partial souls or complexes appeared in these sections autonomously, personified and totally independent of the ego's control. One of the numerous spirits that manifested in these sessions called itself Ivènes and seemed to be an older lady who would offer her advice to people. Jung interpreted this spirit as being a more mature or more developed part of the personality that has not been integrated into consciousness (1902). This is essentially a summary of the notions of the self and of individuation developed by Jung later in his creative work. The self appears here as a potential in the unconscious to be integrated by the conscious mind. Therefore, in his doctorate thesis, Jung's interest in the relationship between the dead and the living is a sort of starting point for the elaboration of the fundamental concepts of his psychology. Jung was disappointed when it was later discovered that his cousin seemed to have lied about the presence of spirits, but he always maintained a keen interest in issues relating to life after death.[6]

From India to the planet Mars

Shamdasani discussed Jung's relationship with the issue of life after death at a conference held by the Jungian Psychoanalytical Association in New York (Shamdasani, 2007). Shamdasani had detected Jung's interest in this theme since his days as a university student in the Zofíngia Club. Still young at the time, he had already referred to the survival of the soul after death using a Kantian reflection. As time and space are both mental categories of perception that are constructed in order to better understand the world, the soul is not subject to these and is able to live on after death. After researching the case of his cousin, Jung maintained a keen interest in supernatural phenomena.

Jung started his systematic research into five mediums from a psychological point of view. In fact, at the beginning of the twentieth century, research by psychologists and psychiatrists into mediums was very common. Many pioneers had carried out psychological investigations into mediums in an attempt to establish significant causal links between the unconscious and the conscious, including Théodore Flournoy, Freud, Ferenzci, Bleuler, William James, Pierre Janet, and Jung himself.[7]

Flournoy was the most important investigator of mediums. His work with the medium Catherine Muller (who became famous under the name "Hélène Smith") was received with enthusiasm when it was published in 1900, entitled *From India to the Planet Mars: A Study of a Case of Somnambulism with Glossolalia*.[8] This title was chosen as Hélène claimed to be the reincarnation of various spirits, including an Indian princess from the fifteenth century and an inhabitant of the planet Mars, whose writing in an unknown alphabet, similar to that of an undiscovered ancient civilisation, Hélène was able to reproduce. Later, the medium started to paint using her psychic powers. Her paintings included beautiful unfamiliar scenes that she claimed were Martian landscapes that she had seen in one of her visions.

Flournoy carried out systematic studies on Hélène Smith's psychic manifestations over five years. Through detailed study of these he demonstrated that they were products of subliminal psychic activity, which is far from the literal approach to spiritual phenomena.

Flournoy was one of the most important precursors of analytical psychology and his (as well as Janet's) influence on Jung's thinking has not yet been given sufficient importance. Flournoy's book is frequently cited by Jung in *Symbols of Transformation* and his theory of subliminal psychic activity can be considered an important precursor to the theory of the collective unconscious.

On life after death

Jung includes various thoughts about the meaning of death at the end of *Memories, Dreams, Reflections*. He writes that he could not theorise on the existence of life after death or the survival of the dead as he was dealing with a limiting concept. On this subject he could only *mythologise*, or tell stories (p. 278). However, the existence of dreams with characters that have died tells us that to a certain extent life does continue after death. He then develops his theory of probable life after death based on the fact that it has been empirically demonstrated that at least a certain part of the psyche escapes the laws of space–time causality (a Kantian return to the ideas he presented at the Zofíngia Club). The various synchronistic phenomena studied by Jung are situated in this sphere.

Based on his experiences during the years he was writing *Liber Novus*, he seeks to demonstrate the continuity of the consciousness after conscious life. In one of his various tales of experiences with people who had already died, Jung mentions in *Memories, Dreams, Reflections* a strange fantasy that he had involving a neighbour who had died the previous day. Having some difficulty sleeping while thinking about the painful loss of his friend, Jung tells how he started to feel unwell, as though there was a very real presence in his room. At first he tried to push away the thought, but then he tried to confront the experience without judging whether it was real or not. He just let his mind flow in the direction it chose and observed the strange presence of his deceased friend. In this fantasy, he followed his friend who headed towards his own house just a few hundred meters away. He went inside and entered the library, walking over to his bookcase. On the top shelf there was a collection of red books by Emile Zola. The dead friend pointed towards the second volume in a series of five. The following day, this strange experience drove Jung to seek his neighbour's widow and ask her permission to visit his library. He saw that on the top shelf there really was a collection of red books by Zola. The title of the second book was: *The Legacy of the Dead* (pp. 289–290).

It is as though this meaningful experience expressed to Jung that the dead have something to say to the living and leave them some form of spiritual legacy, tradition, or genetic heritage to preserve. Perhaps it is this profound truth that led the Ancient Greeks to revere their deified ancestors as *mana* personalities and transform them into mythical hero figures, as these ancestors were responsible for safeguarding old values and transmitting them to new generations.

Ancestors provide the emotional experience of man's basic roots and reinforce a sense of identity. The ancestral spirits that return also bring vital lifeblood and tradition to their people. Heraclitus of Ephesus (Bornheim, 2002) said: "It is delight or death for souls to become wet. We live their death and they our death" (Frag. 77).

We guard the legacy of our ancestors, their tradition, and the seeds that they planted through the generations. We are the guardians and the transformers of these ancestral seeds. This is the legacy that the dead leave us. Past actions, intentions, and desires are all the mental architecture guarded by the family ancestral myth. This legacy is more visible in analytical work relating to parents, childhood memories, secrets, vocations, and parental fantasies, which invisibly mould and pervade the personality through the unconscious. Analysis of our family tree puts us in close contact with the deeper mindsets that span the ages and mould the destinies of entire generations of families.

Jung's approach to the relationship between the dead and the living in *Memories, Dreams, Reflections* is surprising. He values the knowledge of the living in relation to the dead and emphasises life and temporal experience as a space *per se* that can be used for learning and for personal growth. Due to their existence within time and space, the living have a potential for personal development and learning that the dead do not, as they exist within atemporal space. Jung derives these conclusions in *The Red Book* from his encounter with his atemporal inner characters, the old prophet Elijah and the young blind Salome. Jung passed a long time without having any contact with these characters, and when he encountered them again he had the strange sensation that they had changed very little or not at all. The conclusion he reached was that they remained in the archetypal atemporal realm, removed from the historical time associated with the living or conscious life. This meant they had no possibility to learn or transform. Only Jung, as a living (conscious) being can help to remove them from their state of inertia. The characters in *Liber Novus* learn, develop, and begin to understand themselves through their contact with Jung from the temporal realm (p. 284).

This understanding of the important role of the living in relation to the dead originates from one of Jung's crucial dreams, which he also describes in *Memories, Dreams, Reflections*. Great dreams have a fundamental role at certain key moments in Jung's life. This is one of these, and it took place during a bike ride in the city of Ascona in the north of Italy. Jung was travelling with a friend, and they found a place to stay on the banks of Lake Maggiore. They planned to continue their trip through some neighbouring cities before catching the train to Zurich. It was at this time that Jung had a fundamental dream.

> I was in an assemblage of distinguished spirits of earlier centuries; the feeling was similar to one I had later towards the "illustrious ancestors" in the black rock temple of my 1944 vision. The conversation was conducted in Latin. A gentleman with a long, curly wig addressed me and asked a difficult question, the gist of which I could no longer recall after I woke up. I understood him, but did not have a sufficient command of the language to answer him in Latin. I felt so profoundly humiliated by this that the emotion awakened me. (p. 284)

Jung comments that after waking up from this dream he started to reflect on the book he was preparing to write, *Metamorphoses and Symbols of the Libido* (the then title of *Symbols of Transformation*). He had feelings of inferiority in relation to the question that he did not know how to answer. He decided not to continue his trip and returned immediately to Zurich to continue the book he was running behind on. It was only much later that he realised that the old man with the curly wig was an ancestral spirit. The ancestral spirits had been interrogating Jung in order to learn what they had not been able to learn during their own time. It was Jung's task to provide them with the answers, as only he—who lived in three-dimensional space and had a notion of time—could clearly and objectively acquire new knowledge. His role was therefore to teach those living in the atemporal archetypal realm.

This positive vision of the conscious in relation to the unconscious leads Jung to lend excessive value to man in this existential drama. The relationship between man and God is affected by this perspective and was probably a result of his experiences recorded in *The Red Book* and this and other important dreams. God needs man in the same way that man needs God. Man needs God in order to become conscious, and God becomes conscious through man. (See also Jung, 1952, pp. 455–458.) This is of particular importance to man as a conscious being with free will. God in his universality needs man with his reflective conscious in order to become conscious of himself. This is a rather heterodox idea that is far removed from the traditional Christian view and similar to some of the Gnostic formulations that were marginalised by the orthodoxy. Jung later sought support for his perception of the importance of man before God in the medieval mystics (1948a), quoting Angelus Silesius:

> "He cannot live without me,
> nor I without him" (p. 190).

Bringing together the ideas cited above, the hordes of the dead in *Liber Novus* are part of a constant concern that Jung had carried with him since childhood relating to death, transcendence, and the survival of the soul. In *Liber Novus*, Jung seeks to take on the theme of the dead by giving it a symbolic as well as a concrete meaning. This is the fundamental, as the dead start to represent the unlived life and the parts of ourselves that long for conscious expression. Jung, in his final years, gave a final definition of the dead: *those that seek to learn from the living*. In this way he radically inverted the higher knowledge and understanding that is tra-ditionally expected of the dead according to religion and the spiritualist traditions. In addition, although the dead are the guardians of the past and of what is transmitted to us through the generations, they provide us with an incomplete understanding and it is our task to continuously learn and develop both our culture and the generations to come.

CHAPTER EIGHT

The search for the centre

In 1918, Jung was commanding the English section of the hospitalised war wounded at the Chateau-d'Œx in French Switzerland. During this period he systematically drew a range of circular figures he called *mandalas*, a Sanskrit word meaning "magic circles". The psychology of the mandala went on to become one of the main theories of analytical psychology. Jung narrates in *Memories, Dreams, Reflections* that at first he started to spontaneously draw symmetrical concentric circles, and that he noticed that drawing these shapes was a way of objectifying mental content with a high emotional intensity (p. 187). This way he was able to confront and gain a better understanding of the material while keeping himself separate from it. Facing these circular shapes, Jung was performing the process of *active imagination*. (See more on the development of this technique in Chapter Six.) He would later define the mandala as an important symbol of the self. The self as the centre and totality of the psyche could manifest itself in dreams and fantasies in the form of the mandala, expressing the organising and structuring nature of totality.

Mandalas in different cultures

The mandala in its circular and symmetrical form seems to have a calming effect on emotional anxiety. Its spherical shape is an aesthetic representation of the idea of completeness, integrated totality, and the idea of the existence of a centre, which although not clearly marked is at least inferred. Mandalas communicate the idea of the harmonious centralisation of totality. They are normally circular or rectangular in shape, can contain a range of religious representations, and are used across a wide range of cultures for religious or therapeutic purposes. The most widely known mandalas are those from the oriental religions, such as Hinduism and Tibetan Buddhism (see Illustration 2). In this context they have an essentially calming function and can trigger deep states of meditation. Meditation in these religions uses two basic strategies to help deepen the mind: *mantras* and *yantras*. The former are magical sounds that produce specific mental states and the latter are representations or ritual figurations that help the mind to focus and open, enabling creative introspection.

Illustration 2. Tibetan yantra. Image 1 from *Concerning Mandala Symbolism* (Jung, 1950b).
© 2007 Foundation of the Works of C. G. Jung, Zurich.

Oriental monks use the *yantra* mandala in their meditations. The mandalas used in Tibetan and Chinese Buddhism are intricately decorated and represent the entire cosmos. The illustrations involve *Bodhishatvas* and demons and a huge variation of mental states and worlds. Although mandalas are extremely complex, they maintain their circular shape and always direct inwards towards a centre. The monk successively stares at the mandala and tries to mentally repeat its complex symmetrical structure with his eyes closed. The process is repeated various times, and a calm mental state is reached when the mandala is completely visualised in the mind.

The powerful therapeutic influence of the mandala manifests in a wide range of cultures. One of the most widely known examples is the therapeutic use of the mandala by North American Navajo Indians whose shamans draw circular shapes in the sand for healing purposes. The beautiful stained-glass windows of Chartres Cathedral in France are a frequently cited example of religious mandalas in Christianity.[1]

Cultural and psychological mandalas

It is essential that we distinguish the *cultural mandala* from what I call the *psychological mandala*, the latter being described by Jung in his patients dreams and fantasies. The essence of the psychological mandala is the search for a central point, representing a new centre of the personality that is different to the ego, the apparent reference for mental processes. The individuation process described by Jung is the realisation of this virtual centre, which he called the *midpoint of the personality*, existing between the ego and the unconscious. The midpoint of the personality is described in *The Relations between the Ego and the Unconscious* (1928, p. 221). Jung sometimes described the individuation process as a method of "rounding off" (*Abrundung* in German) the personality. This image implies a type of "spherification", with the creation of a new centre, both of which are properties inherent to the mandala. The previously described mandalas are cultural, as they present a strong religious or mythological character, with their images of *Bodhishatvas*, Christian saints, or the rigorous geometry of certain Hindu mandalas created for the worship of a particular deity.

Although the psychological mandala has the same objective as the cultural mandala in centralising the personality and creating emotional stability and depth, it is a subjective and spontaneous manifestation found in dreams and fantasies. In other words, it comes from within in the same way as an archetypal symbol that manifests as part of the collective unconscious. In addition, it does not necessarily have the rich ornamentation of the mandalas that come from the outside world in a specific culture. Tibetan and Christian mandalas belong to a determined ritual and contain specific cultural elements. Their purpose is defined within their specific culture or religious procedure. Psychological mandalas that emerge spontaneously as part of the therapeutic process are entirely autonomous and free of the requirements associated with worship.

At various points, Jung described the spontaneous appearance of psychological mandalas. One of the most important of these citations describes the impressive series of mandalas painted by a North American patient in the 1920s that contained strong archetypal references (1950a). In this series, the individuation process, therapeutic transference, and future aspects of the patient's life appeared in a surprising way. Another notable example is the mandalas that appear in a series of dreams from a patient discussed in *Psychology and Alchemy* (1945). In this case, Jung clearly defines a mandala as a form of spontaneous and automatic expression of the psyche in search of totality. This series of dreams precluded an intense process of psychological transformation. (We know today that the dreamer Jung mentions in *Psychology and Alchemy* is Wolfgang Pauli, the 1946 Nobel prize-winning physicist who collaborated with Jung in his studies on synchronicity.) In the first dream, the initial manifestation of the symbol of the mandala appears in a surprising way: the dreamer finds himself at a party; he is getting ready to leave and sees the image of a stranger's hat he places on his head. Jung amplifies the image of the hat through its association with the king's crown and power, and then expands on the rounded shape of the hat as a manifestation of the mandala, foreshadowing the start of a search for totality (p. 47).

The theme of the hat returns later in dream 35, in which a character picks up a hat and throws it against a wall, leaving behind the circular shape of a mandala divided into eight parts (p. 185).

The image of the mandala also had a strong presence in subsequent dreams, and it was very different to the mandalas of Tibetan Buddhism or the Navajo Indians. In many instances it was not even circular. In one dream, for example, the mandala appears in the form of a large rectangle with smaller rectangles on its edges. In the centre of the larger rectangle is a star and in the middle of each side rectangle is a coloured circle (see dream 51 on p. 192). This demonstrates that the dynamic of it focusing around a centre, which represents the search for centralisation, is more important than it having circular shape. I consider this factor to be significant in order to detect the symbolism of the mandala in the therapeutic process.

The mandala as part of the analytical process

Owing to the fact that the mandala is one of the most important symbols of the self and the archetype of the centre, many hastily believe that its appearance in a patient's fantasies indicates a process of maturation, the integration of opposites, or that the patient is entering into the final process of an analysis. However, this is not always the case. Unconscious symbols should always be approached according to the conscious perspective of the dreamer. When they appear in drawings, dreams, and fantasies, mandalas can actually indicate a psychological crisis or a danger of psychic splitting. In his use of metaphors to compare psychic processes to biological and natural phenomena, Jung started to associate the appearance of psychic mandalas to an increase in leukocytes, the white blood cells (which are also rounded in shape!). A large quantity of white blood cells are produced during infections in order to combat disease and reinstate the body's balance (the so-called "shift to the left" that can be observed on a haemogram). When psychic equilibrium is at risk, the rounded archetype of the self and symbol of totality appears to centre and restore balance.

The radical compensation of mandalas in dissociative states was also researched by Nise da Silveira, founder of the Museum of the Unconscious in Rio de Janeiro (Silveira, 1980). Silveira collected an impressive collection of archetypal images produced by psychotics for the museum. The cataloguing of these images was carried out in conformity with the collection method used at the Archive for Research in Archetypal Symbolism (ARAS)[2] in New York, by which images are catalogued in relation to their archetypal meaning. One of the catalogued themes is the mandala and a range of albums containing images with a mandala theme have been put together. These contain an impressive variety of colours and motifs, all of which express the search for centredness. This significant incidence of mandalas in the drawings of schizophrenics (from *esquizo*, meaning "splitting", and *phrenos*, meaning "mind") is due to the intense *internal splitting* they experience. Healing processes originating from the self attempt to bring these parts together, centralise, and re-establish equilibrium, but the psyche splits again as part of the psychotic process in a tragic repetitive cycle.

I frequently observe mandalas in my clinical practice in both psychotic and non-psychotic patients. One clinical example demonstrates this perfectly. One of my patients with a very complicated family life was living with her widowed mother and two sisters. They were extremely aggressive and the patient often came to her consultations with scratched arms and in a state of silent depression. The consultations often included long moments of silence in which the patient retreated into a melancholic state. On a number of occasions she made mysterious gestures on her knees with her fingers as if she were drawing something. Only after these strange gestures would she look at me and start to speak. In my consultation room I provide crayons, pastels, coloured pencils, and other materials for non-verbal expression. I suggested that she try to draw the shape that she ritualistically designed upon her knee. Illustration 3 was drawn by the patient in red coloured pencil, with violent gestures and little care, and is highly symbolic of her anger and loathing.

Illustration 3. Mandalas and transference.

This is clearly a mandala. Two triangles meet at a central point. This represents the centralisation of the mandala in a non-circular form, with opposites coming together at a central point. The transcendent function of the self is in operation, allowing the patient to organise herself and connect with me through her depressive chaos, verbalise, listen to interpretations, and integrate the entire process. In order for these differentiated mechanisms of analysis to work, the archetype of the self had to manifest in the form of a psychological mandala. A transition was made here from the non-verbal to the verbal, from the depth of the archetypal to more favourable relationship dynamics.

Another clinical example, this time from a psychotic patient, reveals the mysterious and autonomous protective influence that the mandala has over the psyche. One day, a patient of mine suffering from a serious case of bipolar disorder had a major manic episode. He thought he was being followed by dangerous enemy forces. Panic-stricken, he hailed a cab and ordered the driver to drive around the city in search of protection. Finally he told him to stop at a branch of the old National Bank. He paid the fare, got out of the taxi, and stood motionless under the bank's then-famous sign (Illustration 4).

A closer look at this design shows that it is a mandala with a clockwise dynamic movement, which symbolises moving from the unconscious to the consciousness. Perhaps this is why he felt the bank's logo was able to protect him, as it transmits a feeling of the unconscious emptying

Illustration 4. Mandalas and protection.

and the strengthening of consciousness, and this is exactly what the endangered patient needed at that time. In this moment of impending danger, the protection offered by the image of the mandala provided a sort of psychological relief.

This is an interesting example of the transformation of a sign into a symbol. The sign, in this case the unique and well-known logo of a bank, is transformed by the magical thinking of a psychotic into the powerful symbol of the mandala, offering protection against mysterious forces. This phenomenon (the transformation of a sign into a symbol) is the opposite of the more common reduction of symbols into signs, where reductive interpretations are made of symbols in dream analyses. These were highly criticised by Jung.

Oriental mandalas

Writing about the appearance of content from *Liber Novus* in Jung's later work, Shamdasani (2012a) relates the spiralled non-linear way in which the author gradually took ownership of his rich inner experiences and translated them into psychological concepts. In this context, the discovery of the symbolic importance of the mandala has an important resonance in the Chinese alchemic treatise *The Secret of the Golden Flower* (Jung, 1967). Shamdasani refers to this in the following excerpt:

> (…) before taking up alchemy [after finishing *Liber Novus*], we see that Jung engaged in an Eastern intermezzo, which has been somewhat neglected in this regard. The situation becomes clearer if one realises that his commentary on *The Secret of the Golden Flower* is, in many respects, placed in the wrong volume of the *Collected Works*. It shouldn't be in Volume 13, *Alchemical Studies*, but in Volume 11, *Psychology and Eastern Religion*. (p. 368)

Jung's biggest interest when the sinologist Richard Wilhelm sent him this book was not yet alchemy, but the constellation of the mandala, or the circular course of the light as it is called in the treatise. Jung wanted the text to confirm his findings on the importance of the mandala and its association with the symbolism of the self. Only later would the area of alchemy become important to him.

The mandala continued to be an important source of information in his joint research with Wilhelm Hauer on the symbolism of

Kundalini Yoga (Jung, 1999). This Indian tradition represents the chakras as *padmas* (lotus flowers) in the form of mandalas intricately decorated with complex symbolism. A psychological approach to the chakras shows that they involve a sophisticated symbology associated with a specific state of consciousness. In his work with Heinrich Zimmer, a researcher of the Indian religions, Jung reached further into the meaning of the mandala as part of Indian rituals and as an important psychological symbol.

The centralisation of the conscious on the circular *padmas* of the chakras is very interesting from a psychological point of view. The introverted mystics of Indian antiquity intuited these as specific centres of consciousness along the body, and today we recognise these as an important contribution to the understanding of the soul and of unconscious phenomena. After his important "Eastern intermezzo", as Shamdasani named it, Jung started to study yoga and Tantra. His research on the psychological significance of the chakras presented in the Kundalini Yoga seminar are very insightful. The chakras can be understood to be binding mandalas of psychic energy. The location of these mandalas immediately deconstructs the powerful modern fantasy that we only have a cortical conscious. On the contrary, following the Eastern journey that Jung embarked on we can see that there are various levels of consciousness possible and that the cortical conscious of the present-day Western world is just one of the types of consciousness possible. Studying the symbology of the chakras, Jung saw each of these as a universe of consciousness with its own symbolism, number of petals, colours, animal figures, and natural elements. The *manipura chakra*, for example, is situated close to the stomach and the solar plexus. This centre symbolises a type of consciousness governed by automatic reactions and dominated by the fiery emotions. This is the stomach centre where the energies of the gastric juices burn and digest food. When we are "in the stomach" we speak and react in a highly emotional way, our emotions do not reach the level of the heart and we cannot articulate our ideas clearly.[3] Anything can happen when we operate at the level of the stomach, as we react irrationally and fear and aggression often take over. This is an example of how the yogic perspective of there being various centres of consciousness along the body is rich and differentiated, and how it contributes to a new approach to the unconscious. This approach can also be used to overcome the dilemmas of body and mind associated with Western culture.[4]

yjirma mundi totius.

Illustration 5. A mandala for present-day man (*Systema Munditotius*).
From *The Red Book* by C. G. Jung, edited by Sonu Shamdasani, translated by Mark Kyburz, John Peck, and Sonu Shamdasani. Copyright © 2009 by the Foundation of the Works of C. G. Jung Translation 2009 by Mark Kyburz, John Peck, and Sonu Shamdasani. Used by permission of W. W. Norton & Company, Inc.
© 2007 Foundation of the Works of C. G. Jung.

Systema Munditotius: *An inner cosmos in* Liber Novus

The mandala that Jung designed in 1916, which he considered to be his first mandala (Shamdasani, 2012b), was described by Shamdasani as a veritable inner cosmos (see Illustration 5). It uses the formula that Paracelsus developed where the microcosmos replicates the macrocosmos and the inner space of an individual is a miniature cosmos equivalent to the outer cosmos. The *Systema Munditotius* (the system of the whole world) is a whole universe. It is mathematically symmetrical and has a quaternary structure. It brings together the new ideas and intuitions that Jung produced during his confrontation with the unconscious. This mandala is made up of expressive figures from the worlds of Gnosis and classical mythology. As Jung described:

> It portrays the antinomies of the microcosm within the macrocosmic world and its antinomies. At the very top, the figure of the young boy in the winged egg, called Erikapaios or Phanes and thus reminiscent of a spiritual figure of the Orphic Gods. His dark antithesis in the depths is here designated as Abraxas. He represents the *dominus mundi*, the lord of the physical world, and is a world-creator of an ambivalent nature. Sprouting from him we see the tree of life, labelled *vita* ("life") while its upper counterpart is a light-tree in the form of a seven-branched candelabra labelled *Ignis* ("fire") and *Eros* ("love"). Its light points to the spiritual world of the divine child … The accompanying animals of the natural world are a devilish monster and a larva. This signifies death and rebirth. A further division of the mandala is horizontal. To the left we see a circle indicating the body or the blood, and from it rears a serpent, which winds itself around the phallus, as the generative principle. The serpent is dark and light, signifying the dark realm of the earth, the moon and the void (therefore called Satanus) (…) (*Liber Novus*, appendix A, p. 364)[5]

While contemplating the sophisticated cosmology of the *Systema Munditotius* we are transported to the complex symbolism of the mandalas of Tibetan Buddhism. These recreate various worlds, spaces, and dimensions inhabited by a wide variety of beings, Bodhisatvas, gods, and demons representing the various states of being. In the *Systema Munditotius*, doorways to multiple symbolic universes are devised. The elements contained in the mandala are carefully included to represent important moments from *Liber Novus*, meaningful journeys, and experiences as part of a process of self-discovery.

Although it may seem impossible to exhaust the possibilities of the rich symbology of these images, some clues can be picked out that reveal the path taken by Jung through his inner cosmos. Firstly, the mandala performs a role present in every configuration of its type: it orders and centralises. Its strict symmetry had an organising effect on psychological content at a time when Jung was assimilating his unconscious experiences. The unconscious is chaotic by nature and in order to be integrated it needs organising symbols. The *Systema Munditotius* has a quaternary structure involving vertical and horizontal polarities.

On the left of the horizontal polarity are obscure chthonic symbols: the phallus, the serpent, and the earth. On the right there are celestial symbols, the dove of the Holy Spirit, the chalice of the spirit, and the water of life. The vertical polarity also brings together opposites. At the top there is Erikapaios, or Phanes, the celestial youth and the Eros of the ancient Orphic mysteries.[6] At the very bottom is Abraxas, the lord of the world. Above him is the tree of life. In the corresponding position on the upper part of the vertical axis there is a tree of light in the shape of a candelabra. Linked to this tree of light is a winged serpent (representing the arts) and a winged rat (representing the sciences).

Phanes-Eros is the central god of Orphism, a mystical initiatory movement that flourished in Greece during the sixth century BC. According to the Orphic cosmogony, he was born from a silver egg hatched by Nix, the black bird of the night.[7] In the passage describing the encounter with Izdubar, the hatching of the god from an egg and his resurgence in the form of Eros-Phanes express the need for this ancient mythological tradition—personified by Izdubar—to survive in a modern world dominated by one-sided rationality (see Chapter Four). In the *Systema Munditotius*, the supreme god of Orphism has a strong presence. So why does Orphic symbology have such an important role in *Liber Novus*?

To answer this question, the importance of Orphism as a mystery religion in the ancient world must be considered. In order to do this, concepts introduced by the researchers of the ancient religions, particularly Robert Graves, Junito Brandão, and Walter Willi, must be used. The mystery religions included an elaborate ritual based on a myth, the central element being the death of the old personality and the rebirth of a new one. They therefore contained a soteriological element (relating to salvation) for the *mistes*, or initiates. Orphism had very particular characteristics that set it apart from the other mystery religions, such as the Eleusinian and Dionysian rituals. It had a strong Eastern influence and its followers believed in metempsychosis[8] and abstained from eating eggs, which they considered to be the origin of life. It was therefore a rather ascetic religion. Hence, Orphism presented very particular characteristics in comparison to the official Homeric religion of the time. The latter did not involve issues such as individual blame and personal salvation, but placed the blame on the *genos*—the family or social group. The individual could take on the blame of the whole group, and all family members were responsible for the transgressions of its individual members. Any wrong committed by one of the members contaminated the whole group with a *miasma*, (from the Greek, "a spreading stain"). The doctrine of blame and reparation in the official Homeric religion was based on the morality of the family group. The Christian concept of sin still did not exist at the time, but blame and reparation were a hamartia, a word that derives from the verb *hamartanein* meaning "to miss the mark" (Brandão, 1986).

In addition, the official religion of the time did not allow the possibility for post-mortem salvation. On the contrary, Homeric religion included the concept of *Hades* (the world of the dead) where the soul would remain as an abulic double of the living. Orphism, however, included a sophisticated doctrine of personal salvation, and individuals held personal responsibility for their acts and were the master of their own destiny. A highly significant fact in the history of religion is that the notion of individual blame was born in Ancient Greece with Orphism.

According to Junito Brandão, the discovery of the gold tablets in Orphic cemeteries was particularly important in understanding Orphism. These tablets were placed around the neck of the initiate when they died and contained a description of life in the underworld so that they would know the path to follow when leaving the world of the living. The initiate must avoid drinking the water of forgetfulness from the Spring of Lethe. They should instead drink from the Spring of Mnemosyne, which would preserve the memory of their true identity through their previous incarnations. Orphic cosmogony can also be clearly understood through these and other important archaeological discoveries (as well as the Orphic gold tablets, Brandão (1991) cites the Derveni Papyrus as an important source on Orphism, and Walter Willi (1944) acknowledges the existence of a historical Orpheus, founder of a mystery religion at Thrace). The world of Hades was divided into three parts: Tartarus, the lowest part, Erebus, an intermediate part, and the Elysian Fields, a third private part for heroes and important initiates. This concept of the afterlife is strangely similar to the tripartite Christian division of the animic world into Inferno, Purgatory, and Paradise. There are other characteristics belonging to the Orphic movement that lead many to believe that this was an important precursor to Christianity, as it was radically different to the official Homeric religion. In addition, the mythical founder of this movement, the musician Orpheus, was called the fisherman (see Willi, 1944), which is a particularly Christian epithet. The fish is a well-known Christian symbol.

The historical context of Orphism as an important precursor to Christianity could have been attractive to Jung. He was searching for the roots of spirituality in the Western world, threatened by modernity and the "goddess of reason". Perhaps the historical and symbolic significance of the two religious movements of Gnosticism and Orphism explains the important presence of the divinities Phanes and Abraxas in the *Systema Munditotius*. Gnosticism and Orphism are the two systems that synthesise the foundations of Greece and its predecessors in the Judaeo-Christian religion. Jung would have searched these in order to *reculer pour mieux sauter*.[9] He also used this as a new basis with which to systemise his findings from his experiences recorded in *Liber Novus*.

The development of the mandala in Jung's work

The symbology of the mandala has a very significant role in Jung's work and is one of the themes that led to him becoming so well known. In the same way that his other themes became popularised, such as synchronicity and the psychological types, most people do not understand the real meaning of the symbolism of the mandala as a protector of the psyche and an expression of the essential totality of the individual.

We have already considered some important texts on the theme of the mandala in Jung's work: his *Commentary on The Secret of the Golden Flower* (1957), *A Study in the Process of Individuation*, (1950a) and *Concerning Mandala Symbolism* (1950b). However, the development of this theme reaches its climax in his later work *Aion* (1951). In this dense book, a complex series of mandalas appears in perfectly symmetrical form, these being the quaternions that Jung used to describe what he called the structure and dynamics of the self (see Illustrations 6, 7 and 8).

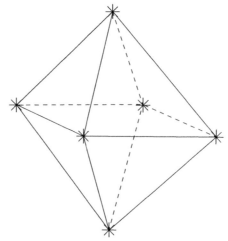

Illustration 6. The Lapis Quaternio.

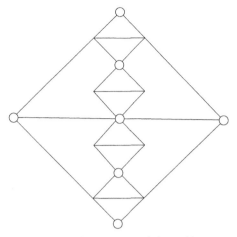

Illustration 7. The symmetrical structure of the self.

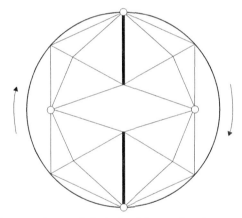

Illustration 8. Quaternios and their final formation into a mandala.

Why did Jung choose quaternions to express the structure of the arche-type of the self? Here it is worth remembering the symbolic importance that Jung gives to the number four throughout his work as a representa-tion of totality, calling this the *quaternion archetype*.

The archetype of the number four appears at various points in Jung's work: the individuation process has four parts, namely the four stages represented by the ego, the shadow, the anima or animus, and the self. Jung also named the four stages of analysis as confes-sion, elucidation, education, and transformation. There are also four psychological functions in Jungian typology and the structure of the

analytical framework is quaternary: the analyst, the analyst's unconscious, the patient, and the patient's unconscious are the frame that
supports the quaternion of the transference. Dreams have a quaternary
structure from a Jungian perspective, comprising presentation, development, climax, and solution. The quaternary structure of dreams follows a basic structure that also appears in the Greek tragedies and in
fairy tales. These have a basic quaternary structure comprising *dra-
matis personae* (description of the characters), development, *peripeteia*
(climax), and *lysis* (solution).

The presence of the number four in the rhythms of nature (the four
seasons, the four phases of the moon, the four primary colours, and the
four cardinal directions, among others) means that the number four
is a fundamental reference in the organisation of human consciousness. It also appears in various traditions across a range of peoples
with marked symbolic significance. The categories of space and time
are the Kantian *a priori* for the organisation of reality. Space, perceived
as ternary with its three dimensions, requires the fourth element, time,
in order to configure space-time totality. Similarly, time, perceived
through past, present, and future requires a fourth element, space, for
the organisation of the totality of the perceived world. In both cases
we have a three-plus-one structure creating a quaternion of perceived
reality (Edinger, 1996).

The sophisticated structure used by Jung to describe the archetype of
the self in *Aion* can be considered to be a mandala unfolding on various
levels in subjective and objective space. Jung bases this on the complex
thinking of the Gnostic school of the *Naassenes* and its wealth of images
to illustrate what would become the basic structure of the archetype of
the self. The Naassenes (meaning "the snake worshippers", according to
some etymologies, from the Greek *naas*, meaning "snake") were a group
of Gnostic thinkers from the first century whose traditions became known
through the writings of the bishop Hippolytus. Hippolytus's texts on
the Naassenes are cited at length by Jung at various points of his *Collected Works*, principally in *Aion*. The Naassenes belonged to the group of
Gnostics called the Ophites (from the Greek *ofis*, meaning "snake") who
attributed a libertarian role to the snake of paradise, which recued man
from a cruel Jehovah so he could gain consiousness. Psychologically, the
Gnostic snake can be considered to be a personification of the anima.
The Gnostic sources that Jung researched contain a rich symbology and
interesting interpretations of Old Testament, primitive Christian, and

Greek texts, bringing together these traditions and expressing powerful symbols using wordplay. According to Edinger (1996), this way of expressing symbols using wordplay is very similar to the structure of the dreams of contemporary man.

I consider it important that the complex symmetrical structure of the self be seen in the final unfolding of the *Systema Munditotius* in *Liber Novus*, Jung's initial intuitive perception of the mandala. Here the idea is still being formed, and its culmination can be seen in *Aion*, where it is organised into a theoretical system that can be used to perceive both man and the world, and in which Gnosticism, Orphism, and alchemy are the basic references.

CHAPTER NINE

Philemon

In his book of memoirs Jung wrote: "Philemon and other figures of my fantasies brought home to me the crucial insight that there are things in the psyche which I do not produce, but produce themselves and have their own life" (1963, p. 176).

The appearance of Philemon represents the culmination of Jung's pilgrimage in search of the self. Philemon is referred to in *Memories, Dreams, Reflections* as equivalent to the guru figure in Indian religion. Jung relates how he had a real-life experience with a guru when he was visited by an Indian intellectual who was one of Gandhi's disciples. The visitor revealed that he had had a guru, and Jung asked him who this was. He answered that his guru was called Sankaracharya. Jung was surprised: "You don't mean the commentator on the Vedas who died centuries ago?" His visitor then explained "matter-of-factly" that this was not at all relevant and that the guru experience is an inner experience. At that moment, said Jung, "I thought of Philemon" (p. 177).

The word guru has been overused in recent times and is often used incorrectly. There are various etymologies for this Sanskrit word, and the most commonly known of these defines it as a person who leads you from the darkness (*Gu*) into the light (*Ru*), a highly qualified spiritual master or a "dissipater of darkness". Another etymological explanation is that it is a cognate of the Latin *gravis*, meaning "heavy" or "full" (of wisdom and divine knowledge). Tradition reveals the formula: guru, god, self, identical experiences.[1] Therefore, this comparison of Philemon with the guru figure places it in the category of the archetype of the wise old man, an important teacher for Jung.

Indeed, Philemon is compared to an avatar through a citation from the *Bhagavad Gita*, the sacred Hindu book belonging to the *Upanishads*. Jung placed the following citation next to a picture of Philemon in *Liber Secundus*:

> Whenever and wherever a decline of righteousness and a predomi-nance of unrighteousness prevails; at that time I manifest myself personally. For the protection of the devotees and the annihilation of the miscreants, and to fully establish righteousness, I appear millennium after millennium. (Chapter 4, verses 7–8)

In the psychodynamics of individuation, the *avatar* represents an unconscious factor responsible for re-establishing the balance lost by the conscious personality. "Whenever there is a decline of righ-teousness" means that when the conscious is disorientated, symbols of the self (the wise old man as an avatar, for example) appear to help the conscious to recover its lost equilibrium. This new equilibrium is always more advanced and exists on a higher plane. Crises are a call-ing for psychological development. People can often have difficulty entering into contact with the wise old man in themselves and project this figure onto their analyst as part of the transference. It is vital that the analyst embodies the archetypal image (temporarily) for the cli-ent until the client can integrate the values it represents when he is ready and no longer needs to project this idealised image onto the therapist.

Jung makes references to Indian culture throughout *Liber Novus*.[2] The *Collected Works* are full of references to Hinduism, such as in Volume 11, *Psychology and Eastern Religion*, and in Volume 6, *Psycho-logical Types*, where the *Vedas* and *Upanishads* are cited at length. There are also the *Kundalini Yoga* seminars given by Jung and Wilhelm Hauer.

Jung's journey to India and his work on the contribution of this culture are part of his wider interest in man on a planetary and cross-cultural basis. This approach is still significant today at a time when multiple cultures are coming together.

In *Memories, Dreams, Reflections*, Jung explains that the figure of Philemon is an unfolding of the figure of Elijah and a continuation of the same principle (p. 175). How should this be interpreted? It is worth remembering that *Liber Novus* is a constant personification of emotions, and that if these had not been differentiated they could have been dangerous for the conscious. When these chaotic emotions acquire an image or are personified, they can be integrated into the conscious. The archetype of the spirit, the principle of feeling, initially appears in *Liber Primus* in the form of a spontaneous, autonomous thought. *The Spirit of the Depths* is then personified as Elijah and later takes on the form of Philemon. These personifications are successive differentiations of the same archetypal principle. This spiritual principle is later conceptualised by Jung as the archetype of the spirit, the archetype of the wise old man, or the *principle of reflection* (1948b, pp. 35, 37).

The first time that Philemon appears, similarly other important events in Jung's life, is in a dream. He appears flying through a sky as blue as water and full of flat clods of earth. He has wings like those of a kingfisher, holds in his hand a bunch of keys, one of which he is clutching as if about to open a lock, and has the horns of a bull. He brings Jung, in his own words, "a strange Egypto-Hellenic atmosphere with a Gnostic colouration", unlike Elijah, a Jewish prophet from the Old Testament (1963, p. 176).

At first, Jung doesn't completely understand the symbolic meaning of Philemon and cultivates his image, keeping it alive and observing the different meanings for it appearing in his imagination. He kept this image of Philemon alive using his tempera painting (see Illustration 9).

This image is one of the best-known paintings in *Liber Novus*. The venerable countenance of Philemon has a strange similarity to Jung's own face at the end of his life. Each element of this image has a different symbolic meaning and merits separate analysis. The bird's wings are present in the personification found in Western mysticism as a symbol of transcendence and transport.[3] Angels, the quintessential winged beings, get their name from the Greek *angelos*, meaning "messenger". Angels are heralds, the messengers between man and God. The Greeks' messenger god was Hermes, with his winged sandals. In addition,

Illustration 9. Philemon.
From *The Red Book* by C. G. Jung, edited by Sonu Shamdasani, translated by Mark
Kyburz, John Peck, and Sonu Shamdasani. Copyright © 2009 by the Foundation
of the Works of C. G. Jung Translation 2009 by Mark Kyburz, John Peck, and Sonu
Shamdasani. Used by permission of W. W. Norton & Company, Inc.

Hermes is described as a *psychopomp*, meaning "the guide of souls"
(from *psyche*, meaning "soul", and *pompos*, meaning "guide"). Wings
are therefore associated with transport and communication, which is
one of Philemon's roles.

Another important symbolic element in Philemon is his bull's horns
(present in the dream that Jung relates in *Memories, Dreams, Reflections*
but substituted in the painting in *The Red Book* with an analogous
luminous halo). The horns were a symbolic representation of power
in pre-Christian cultures. They were used as an ornament by figures
of authority and religious chiefs. They also bring a feeling of prosper-
ity and abundance. In a way, these horns reinforce Philemon's spiritual authority.

The keys express the idea that Philemon is a figure containing many meanings that are yet to be identified. Only through continuous study of the symbols can the unconscious reveal these new meanings.

Philemon is carrying a small flame and its opaque light is reflected onto his chest. This small flame can be seen in various representations of figures of the unconscious, symbolising a new potential conscious present in the unconscious. This is Paracelsus's *lumen naturae* ("the light of nature"), the range of possibilities for development present in the unconscious. This is an important perspective, as the unconscious is no longer purely negative or simply a repository for repressed material. Here it is seen as a source of creativity and of coming into being. Philemon carrying the small flame may have also been reported by Von Franz studying Jung's dream (1975), where it was named the "the storm lantern". In this dream, Jung carries a dim lantern close to his chest on choppy seas during a bad storm. Von Franz (pp. 40, 41) sees the dim light of the lantern as a representation of the conscious that needs to be preserved at any cost. This dream reminded Jung of the importance of the conscious in the confrontation with the unconscious. Indeed, the ethical position of the conscious is fundamental in active imagination and in all the experiences documented in *Liber Novus*, in which the most surprising, obscure, and unusual content appears. We need to adopt a middle ground in which this content is confronted without it being repressed in favour of conscious logic, but where it is not identified with, confusing the conscious. A firm conscious and critical position is required. Using Jung's dream as a reference, Philemon represents Jung's self, his supraordinate personality, and the dim light that he carries close to his chest is his egoic conscious. Seen from this perspective, the figure of Philemon represents not just the self, but is also a poetic and mystical representation of the ego-self axis, or the interaction and the interdependence of both these parts of the psyche.

Philemon's infirmitas

One of the most significant characteristics of Philemon is his feet. Jung relates that Philemon has a lame foot (1963, p. 178). Is this what Hillman called the *"infirmitas* of the archetype" (1980, pp. 1–5)? Perhaps so, as figures of the unconscious do appear with their infirmitas, as though the gods had ailments that represented various ways of the soul manifesting its imperfections, similar to Hillman's proposal that pathologising may be a spontaneous movement of the soul. In the same way that Salome is blind and that this is an issue for Jung, Philemon's lame foot has implications for his individuation process. Salome's blindness is cured at the end of *Liber Primus* in a moment of great transformation. Psychodynamically speaking, Jung's anima undergoes a transformation. One of the "lowly", a shadowy figure that accompanies Jung at certain points of *Liber Secundus*, has lost one of his eyes in a fight. In this case, however, the infirmitas seems to indicate the limited consciousness that is part of the human condition, known in the East as *avidya*, meaning "not knowing", the ignorance of the conscious being (Eliade, 1962, p. 33). Philemon's foot is never cured, but this infirmitas is compensated for with the appearance of another figure of the unconscious.

The appearance of Ka, the soul of the Pharaoh

Jung assumes that Philemon is an *angelos*, a spirit of the air representing "the superior insight" (1963, p. 176). Although he has enormous wings with the colour of a kingfisher's, he also has a lame foot. Philemon is put into context to a certain extent by the later appearance of another character, whom Jung calls Ka. This name derives from ancient Egypt, where it was believed that man possessed various souls, including the *Ka*, which was the soul linked to the body and the material world in general. Incidentally, Ronald Hayman hypothesises—without explanation—that the name Ka is a corruption of Jung's own name, Carl! This is an extreme example of how hypotheses can be made with absolutely no basis in concrete facts (2002, p. 183).

In Jung's active imagination, Ka appears from a deep well from the depths of the earth. This is in contrast to the appearance of Philemon, who appears from the air. Jung compares Ka to the metal spirit of the alchemist, which is playful yet also Mephistophelian in its mystery. While Philemon brings with him the spiritual question of meaning, Ka brings with him the "principle of beauty", or the "eternal reflection in material".[4]

Jung also worked with the image of Ka in a painting. This was Jung's usual way of carrying out what he called his *circumambulatio*, meaning the circling of a symbol.[5] Drawing, sculpting, painting, or writing about an image was his revolutionary way of keeping the flame of his mysterious experiences alive without reducing them to hasty rational interpretations. This process is the essence of the unfolding of *Liber Novus*.

Ka, in the same way as Philemon, gains symbolic expression through a painting, in which he appears standing on the ground surrounded by earth, beside a stone altar with a bronze top. At the top of the painting there is a kingfisher's wing and between this and his head there is a nebula of stars. Ka is holding a stylus and is working on a shrine. He says, "I am he who buries the Gods in gold and gems."[6]

This painting clearly shows that Philemon and Ka complement one another, representing two complementary areas of the psyche that together can achieve individuation. Philemon is above, represented by his wing, and Ka is below, carrying out his creative work. The nebula of stars between the two represents Jung's constellation of the self and the creation of new potential (the stars) through the integration of opposites.

The myth of totality was central to Jung's life and guided his entire theory. The idea of totality is present in the question of the psychological types and the inferior function, and in his concepts linked to the self as a pair of complementary opposites. It is evident that Jung's work integrated his opposing elements throughout his lifetime. As he himself commented on various occasions, his main psychological functions were always thinking and intuition (personified by Philemon). His work with the psychological function of sensation (personified by Ka) was a constant in his life, with his search to live a life in harmony with nature. He never installed electricity or any other present-day facilities in the Bollingen Tower, and he tried to live there alongside Mother Nature, cutting wood, tending to the fire, and cooking. He channelled Ka's creative energy as a creative artist, sculptor, and painter, "he who buries the Gods in gold and gems".

CHAPTER TEN

Final conclusions

"*The Red Book* is like the god Janus as it has two sides: one that looks to the past, is traditional and medievalist, and the other that contemplates future developments in psychological theory and practice."

Seven years after the publication of *Liber Novus*, we are now able to evaluate its influence on Jungian psychology and contemporary psychology in general. The book is a very unique and original psychological reference. After its publication in 2009, numerous events across the world have been held in order to research, disseminate, and debate the various aspects of *Liber Novus* and its significance for Jungian psychology. At the same time, as we dive into the book and discuss its various aspects, it is fascinating to see Jung's concepts as they are being formed, their origin in intense subjective experiences, and their gradual condensation into the theoretical body of Jung's work.

This book discusses the immediate meaning of *Liber Novus* (see Chapter One), a creative and emotionally intense journey that Jung took in order to face his midlife crisis. Although this midlife crisis was a very important factor in the production of the book, *Liber Novus* should be considered to be a part of Jung's existential process in general. *Liber Novus* represents a continent of varied impressions from the personal life of its author that at the time had still not been completely understood by his conscious. It contains symbolic representations of various philosophical, religious, and existential questions that had tormented Jung since his childhood. The large number and variety of symbols that emerged at this time were gradually and continuously integrated through creative processes along the course of his life.

The process of assimilating these intense experiences lends *Liber Novus* a true significance in the genesis of the author's work. It clearly identifies his first conceptualisations on the individuation process and the various inner characters that are involved in this. The stages of the process, the encounters with the shadow, the anima, and the symbolic representations of the self are clearly described. The identification of these concepts and the description of the process in general are achieved through personification.

The Red Book *and a civilisation in transition*

The Red Book was written at a time when the West was undergoing a radical cultural crisis. Changes in Western civilisation began in the eighteenth century with the start of the Industrial Revolution. The book was written as the First World War was breaking out and alongside the deep cultural transformations that it caused. These affected a wide range of human activities across the arts, the sciences, and human culture in general. A paradigm shift took place that had a deep cultural impact. At the start of the twentieth century, new radical ideas were being introduced by Albert Einstein, such as the theory of relativity in 1906, the same year in which Jung published *The Psychology of Dementia Praecox*, Freud completed his *Three Essays on the Theory of Sexuality*, and Picasso painted the first cubist painting, *les Démoiselles d'Avignon*.

Picasso's style of painting is related to the cultural revolution that took place during the first decade of the last century, as cubism employed multiple perspectives. Paintings from the Middle Ages were drawn on a single plane, and the first painter to break way from this was the Renaissance artist Leonardo da Vinci using his *sfumato* technique. Cubism offers multiple possibilities of visualisation. This multiplicity is similar to the symbolic vision and perspective of the unconscious that the new discipline of psychoanalysis introduced by

Freud and Jung provided. It is also worth remembering that the models that Picasso used were prostitutes from the city of Avignon, prohibited as a result of the repressed sexuality that Freud studied.[1]

It is worth remembering that *Liber Novus* came about during a moment of crisis when all the cultural references of the time were undergoing a profound transformation. This happened at the beginning of the twentieth century when significant cultural changes in the sciences and arts were taking place. At the same time, various movements were reacting to the unilateralism of Europe's scientific materialism. The Dadaism movement, founded in Zurich in 1916, represented a vigorous protest against the excesses of modern rationality.[2]

A range of other religious and philosophical movements opposing modernity appeared. One group of intellectuals and artists inaugurated a place where people could worship the cult of nature that they called *Monte Veritá* (the Mountain of Truth), close to the small city of Ascona on the banks of Lake Maggiore on the Swiss-Italian border.[3] Jung had connections with some participants of Verita' Mountain ("Moutain of Truth"). Some of the participants were Hermann Hesse, the psychiatrist Otto Gross, the dance researcher Laban and the German writer awarded the Nobel prize in 1912 Gerhardt Hauptmann. One of Hauptmann's best-known books talks about the spirit of Monte Veritá. His novel *The Heretic of Soana* became famous across the whole of Europe (1918). Hauptmann narrates the story of the young Father Francisco who is transferred to the village of Soana and falls in love with the beautiful Agata, who is the product of an incestuous relationship. It is an erotic story providing a harsh criticism of empty Christianity that proposes a return to a pagan religion based on naturalism. The young Agata is described at the end of the book as a goddess of nature with the beauty and power of a great mother. At this point it is clear that the book is proposing a redemption and return to pre-Christian values. Blavatsky's ideas on theosophy, vegetarianism, and Eastern religion also had an important role for the movement at Monte Veritá. All of these issues emerged as a form of compensation against the materialistic values of the Industrial Revolution that had swept over Europe.

These movements oscillating between the rational and the irrational, science and art and science and religion, are cultural flows that continue to this day and could well go on forever, like some form of psychological necessity within the cultural unconscious. Sanford Drob suggests that *The Red Book* also has a compensatory function in relation to current psychological techniques biased towards the rational approach (2012). According to Drob, the influence of neuroscience and behavioural techniques in present-day psychotherapy is extremely one-sided and *The Red Book* proposes an approach in which the imagination and the irrational can also be included.

I believe that the various existing ways of approaching the psyche do not invalidate the Jungian model involving the archetypes and the cultivation of images. These alternative models of approach can coexist within the current paradigm. Edgar Morin (1999) proposes the name *of paradigm of complexity* to new emerging paradigm. As he comments, the word *complexus* means "to weave together". He explains his choice of the word *complexity* as follows:

> Knowledge, under the authority of the brain, separates and reduces. We reduce man to an animal, to the physical-chemical (…). The key issue is the thought that unites, and for this reason the word complexity is so important in my opinion, as *complexus* means "that which is woven together", giving character to the tapestry. (1999, pp. 21–34)

Recent efforts to research and map the brain over the next ten years (known as the Human Connectome Project, a name that makes reference to the "simpler" (!) Human Genome Project) does not fully invalidate the approach using the symbolic and the imagination. Alongside the development of biological approaches, laboratory research has demonstrated the efficiency of meditation and eating natural foods in the prevention of a range of psychological and physical problems. For example, the neuro-psychiatrist Servant-Schreiber tried to develop a method for treating cancer based on natural medicines, meditation, and physical exercise associated with conventional biomedical treatments (2007). This demonstrates the possibility of creatively integrating these different approaches.

The global dynamism of this crisis of transformation is naturally intensified by the speed of communications through the internet and through intense cultural exchanges between people who are geographically very far from one another. Part of this movement of change includes an exacerbated scientism dominating some areas of knowledge. The progress of neuroscience has brought with it new perspectives for the study of the personality. Despite the huge achievements in this field, however, relationships between the mind and the body-brain are still to be explored. What is the exact relationship between the brain (a structure) and the mind (a process)? How do neuron structures, synapses, and chemical reactions link with thoughts, philosophical ideas, the imagination, and feelings such as altruism and solidarity? Satisfactory answers have still not been found for these questions.[4] Similarly, the unconscious and the psyche as a whole cannot be grasped using purely experimental methods or laboratory experiences. This is despite the huge emphasis put on the biological model in the United States and Europe in recent years.

Just as *Liber Novus* was written at a time of great cultural change, I consider it highly significant that it has been made available to the public so many years later, during another period of transition. It was in the symbolic year of 2000 that the Society of Heirs to the Work of Jung authorised the publication of *The Red Book*. Similarly to the time that the book was written, this period was also characterised by an intense cultural crisis.

The year 2000 represented an age full of symbolism and fantasies relating to the turn of the millennium. Millenarianism, the archetypal idea that the destiny of humanity or of groups of humans is intimately linked to the passing of time and the changing of ages, has existed since ancient times. Visionaries, prophets, and shamans from all periods of human history spoke of millennial events that would bring salvation or condemnation and damnation.

Jung himself was interested in the millenarianist Cistercian monk Joachim de Fiora, who lived in Italy in the seventh century (Jung, 1951, pp. 82 ff.). Fiora preached a millenarianist doctrine, according to which the millennium before Christ belonged to the Father, the millennium of Mosaic Law and obedience through fear; the first millennium AD belonged to the Son, an era based on faith and love; and the second millennium AD would belong to the Holy Spirit. The influence of the Holy Spirit would determine the predominance of the monastic orders, meditation, and the inner life, marked by an introspective attitude as opposed to a strong traditional institutional influence.

Once again, from the year 2000 a range of millennial fantasies erupted within the collective imagination, some of which were very strange, including predictions from a certain Mayan calendar and the technological theory known as the Millennium Bug. According to the latter, none of the computers based on the digital system would be able to operate as a result of the three zeros in the new date. This fear that technology would fail seems like child's play compared to the political and social events that unfolded from the year 2000 onwards.

The new millennium was seen in with the attack on the Twin Towers in New York on September 11, 2001, signalling the start of a new era of transformation for civilisation as we know it. The year 2002 was a year of the god Janus, the ancient Roman god of gateways, who had two faces. It was also what numerologists call a palindromic year, for which the start and end are a mirror image of each other (20-02) and symmetrical opposites confront one another. This was a time of radical confrontation between opposites; the new, the renewable, the disposable, and the culture of information technology that is updated almost on a monthly basis, *vs.* the traditional and medieval cultures of the Middle East upholding permanent and unchanging lip values. Is it possible for these two opposites to come together?

At this time of crisis and of millenarianist expectations, *Liber Novus* was finally published by the Philemon Foundation in 2009. *The Red Book* is also a Janus book, as it has two faces, very much in keeping with the period of transition in which it was published. One face looks to the past and is traditional. Even the book's appearance is linked to the past, seemingly written on medieval papyrus with gothic letters and tempera adornments and illustrations. The book discusses the beginnings of Christianity in the desert, when Jung talks to Ammonius the Anchorite, who was alive during the first centuries of the age of Christ. Figures from the Old Testament, Ancient Greece, and other societies from antiquity are also present. The encounter with Izdubar speaks of the need to establish a link with ancient cultures and the mythological thinking that has been abandoned by modernity and its goddess of reason.

The Red Book has another face, however, which is a face that looks ahead to the future, suggesting new ways forward and approaches for psychological theory and psychotherapy. I would summarise the new approaches contained within *The Red Book* into the following four categories: the personification of emotions, the concept of the self and the individuation process, the concept of the objective psyche, and finally the practical results of these new perspectives, which provide a new form of Jungian psychotherapy redesigned as a result of the author's personal experiences.

Personifying emotions

Faced with personal images that appear in great intensity, it seems clear that giving a shape to these unidentifiable emotions was a fundamental factor in their gradual integration by Jung. We can see that the more abstract emotions and tendencies are worked through little by little as the book progresses, becoming more defined through the process of personification (see Chapter Three). The *Spirit of the Depths*, the factor that led Jung to his inner experience, first manifests as a voice, a calling, and an inclination. Only at the end of *Liber Primus* is this personified as the prophet Elijah, and later on in the second part of *Liber Secundus* and in "Scrutinies" as Philemon. These successive personifications allow a gradual integration of this content. The whole of *Liber Novus* has a double structure, the first involving direct emotional experiences associated with certain images and the second involving a more rational elaboration. Here experience becomes theory and theory becomes the method. Using his fundamental experiences, Jung organises a new psychological theory based on personified images and his individuation process.

The concept of the self and the individuation process

Using the experiences he describes in *Liber Novus*, Jung coherently organised in his theory the intuition of the existence of a second centre of psychic life other than the ego: the self. This intuition was central to his life and had appeared at various moments since he was a child, when he sat on a rock close to his house and asked himself, "Is it me sitting on the stone thinking about it, or am I being thought by the stone?" (1963, p. 33). He also had fantasies when he was young that at the same time as being a normal young boy, he was also an old man that dressed in clothes from the eighteenth century (p. 55). *Liber Novus* helped Jung to organise this concept theoretically. Individuation was to be a process used to seek a new form of psychological organisation based on a new centre within the personality: the self.

Through these intuitions and personal experiences, Jung coherently establishes a theoretical identity related to his thinking. The notion of the self as a centre and at the same time the totality of the conscious and unconscious psyche differentiates it from traditional psychoanalysis. Soon after his separation from Freud, at the time that he started to write *Liber Novus*, Jung emphasised that his concept of the unconscious was different to Freud's, as he saw it just as a deposit for repressed material. The unconscious was an epiphenomenon—something derived from the conscious and not an entity in itself. The Jungian notion presumes that the unconscious is a creative *a priori*, full of archetypal images. However, the psychoanalysis that Jung criticised belonged to Freud's first topic, with the psyche divided into the conscious, the preconscious (where subliminal processes are located), and the unconscious. After *The Ego and the Id* was published in 1923, Freud began his second topic, which involved his structure of the id, the ego, and the superego. According to this view, the id as an unconscious structure comes before the conscious. Therefore, Freud's concept of the structure of the mind is similar to the Jungian model, in which the unconscious is a primary phenomenon. For Freud, however, the id was always a bundle of drives without direction. With the notion of the self that originated from his experiences in *Liber Novus*, Jung introduces the notion of the unconscious having a different order to the ego, with the function of a prospective organisation in the future, making this a teleological function. Noticing a type of organisation in his fantasies, dreams, and paintings that was different to that of the conscious intention of the ego, he conceived the self as an organising centre of the psyche as a whole. At the same time, Jung conceptualised the self as the totality of conscious and unconscious psychological processes. Analysing a series of his own and his patients' dreams, Jung could observe this process of the self in action, moving towards individuation.

Liber Novus provided Jung with a basis from which he could solidify his theory of the personality, grounded in the finalistic processes organised by the self. During these processes, psychic energy is personified in a constant dialectic with conscious processes.

The objective psyche

One of Jung's most fundamental lessons during his inner journey in *The Red Book* was given by the prophet Elijah and later by Philemon on the objective aspects of the deeper layers of the unconscious. When meeting the divine figures of Elijah and Salome, Jung was perplexed by the proximity between a saintly prophet from the Old Testament and the sinful Salome, responsible for the decapitation of John the Baptist. Seeking a rational explanation for this mystery, he initially interprets Elijah as representing the more differentiated psychological function of thought, and Salome, the beautiful blind girl, as representing the less differentiated function of feeling. He then seeks another way to interact with these figures, using the method that he would later call *amplification*: the image of a wise old man with a young girl became a typical way of personifying the psychic energy of the collective unconscious, in the same way that this is done through fairy tales in which the old man and princess coupling is often observed. Gnostic legend has its figure of Simon Magus and the young Helena, and in alchemy there is the example of the adept working together with his soror mystica.

Surprisingly, Elijah reacts to Jung's rational interpretations:

I [Jung]: "What my eyes see is exactly what I cannot grasp. You, Elijah, who are a prophet, the mouth of God, and she [Salome], a bloodthirsty horror. You are the symbol of the most extreme contradiction."

Elijah: "We are real and not symbols" (p. 246).

And later:

Elijah: "You may call us symbols for the same reason that you can also call your fellow men symbols, if you wish to. You invalidate nothing and solve nothing by calling us symbols."

I: "You plunge me into a terrible confusion. Do you wish to be real?"

Elijah: "We are certainly what you call real. Here we are, and you have to accept us. The choice is yours" (p. 249).

This passage demonstrates what Jung would establish in his work as the reality of the soul. The psychological events are real, and they have the same status as any objective reality. Starting to formulate this, Jung then proposes a layer of the psyche that he names the *objective psyche*, which is autonomous and conscious in nature and present in the unconscious. The theoretical elaboration of these experiences belonging to the reality of the psyche is only achieved much later in Jung's later work.[5] The complex concept of the *objective psyche* or the reality of the soul paves the way for a new epistemology for the mental phenomena. According to Jung, psychic content is real as long as it exists. It operates and is effective though the experience of the psyche. In addition, psychological content has an objective existence and is not a mere epiphenomenon of the conscious psyche. This epistemological turnaround is echoed in modern physics where the rigid discrimination between subject and object falls down. Jung reflects on these findings of a conscious within the unconscious in his later work, discussing the autonomous conscious content of the unconscious that operates independently of free will. With this proposition, the traditional structure of the psyche, polarised between the layers of the conscious and the unconscious, is called into question. This is because the term unconscious contains the remnants of its historical discovery, according to which it is seen as the absence of consciousness.

The conscious–unconscious opposition is one of the great polarisations that dominate our culture and help to organise the modern paradigm. Since humanity created its first polarisation between man and nature, civilisation has been organised according to polarities: civilised and tribal, conqueror and conquered, the northern and southern hemispheres, male and female, the spiritual and the material, and soul and body, among others. These polarisations are always hierarchical and rigid, which is a serious matter indeed as men are seen as superior to women, the soul to the body, the spiritual to the material, the civilised to the tribal, and so on.[6] Within the polar structure of conscious and unconscious, there will always be some form of hierarchy by definition, with the unconscious being seen as lacking, the absence of consciousness placing it from the start as inferior to the conscious. If we follow the history of the unconscious, we see that psychopathology, symptoms, and lack of social acceptance were always the route to its discovery. For this reason, the unconscious consistently manifested itself via the psychopathologies. However, this perception of the unconscious as inferior does not do it justice, as it is a fundamental creative force in the human experience. The unconscious is always at work in the arts, the sciences, and in any creative pursuit.

When Jung defends the unconscious as a value in itself through his experiences described in *Liber Novus*, showing that it has its own autonomy, creativity, and meaning (the *Spirit of the Depths* personified as Philemon), it is no longer un-conscious and the term becomes inadequate. This is why Jung proposed the term *objective psyche* to describe a layer of the psyche universal to all of humanity, with its own objectivity and autonomy and no longer an epiphenomenon derived from the conscious, inferior to the lucid and rational conscious.

A new psychotherapy

It is said that psychoanalysis and depth psychology (including all the schools of psychotherapy that take the unconscious into consideration) are undergoing a crisis. In reality, it seems as though the crisis lies with the traditional model of psychoanalysis, which involves various consultations per week and takes large periods of time. We need to be open to new and more agile approaches that use the wide range of expressive techniques proposed by Jung as a result of his own experience with *Liber Novus*.

In any psychotherapeutical journey using the unconscious as a reference and within the parameters of any school of thought, we follow two processes in parallel: on one hand it is important that we have some kind of theoretical and operational reference so that this process does not take place in the dark and purely through intuition. On the other hand, the therapeutic process will always involve a direct emotional encounter between two people. Jung always affirmed that the personality of the therapist is essential to ensure cure. He once cited an old alchemical dictum, "Art requires the whole man" (1945, p. 6). *The Red Book* is a powerful affirmation that personal experience is fundamental in the process of psychological cure. The book also relates the therapeutic process of Jung himself. This process has nothing to do with the conventional cure for symptoms, and is much more like a total transformation of the personality. Symbolic experiences are the central process in cure and transformation, the results of which are unpredictable and the duration undetermined. It is a process that is out of the control of the conscious and which cannot be planned. It is constructed in each moment, the wanderer taking his personal path and the transformations taking place with each step.

Liber Novus contains the basis of a form of Jungian therapy based on the technique of active imagination. As a result of his encounters with inner characters, Jung developed a new and highly creative way of working with the unconscious. He summarised this process for the first time in his work *The Transcendent Function*, written at the same time as *Liber Novus*. The foundations for a new attitude towards analysis are elaborated in *Liber Novus*, and non-verbal expressive techniques are an important part of this process.

Based on his experience, the technique of working with images, paintings, drawings, and sculpture is highly valued by Jung himself and by his collaborators. Working with dreams and images is fixed at the centre of the Jungian model. The C. G. Jung Institute Zurich has put together a *Bild Archiv* (image archive) for the systematic research of archetypal images in paintings and artistic production in general.

Subsequent generations of Jungian analysts have sought to integrate the model of dream interpretation and expressive techniques developed by Jung in *Liber Novus* using a systematic approach, involving a Jungian therapeutic setting and the interpretation of transference. An archetypal transference model has been developed, as well as studies on the primary relationship between mothers and their babies and the influence of this on psychopathology. I consider the notion of archetypal transference to be fundamental to the therapeutic process. Transference is always present and must be recognised by any therapist. However, it contains archetypal images and has a purpose and meaning within the analytical process. Many authors have sought to integrate Jung's theory with that of other psychoanalytic authors. Within this hybrid model, the use of active imagination and the personification of archetypal figures are both still important in the understanding of the individuation process and the evolution of the therapeutic process.

Finalising the book

Regarding the results and the duration of this process, we must not forget that Jung toiled over *The Red Book* for sixteen years. He left it incomplete, in the middle of a sentence, when he tried to go back to it in 1959. In this year, Jung tried to complete *The Red Book* but did not succeed. At the end of page 190 of his calligraphed copy he ended with an incomplete phase: "I knew how frightfully inadequate this undertaking was, but despite much work and many distractions I remained true to it, even if another possibility never". Was Jung was successful in relation to his self-analysis?

We can say that he was, that he did not get lost among the various symbols of the book, and that this lay the foundations for his posterior theoretic work and his work on himself. Jung stated that he stopped working on *The Red Book* in 1928 when he discovered alchemy upon receiving a copy of the Chinese alchemic treatise *The Secret of the Golden Flower* from the sinologist Richard Wilhelm. However, there is no doubt that he already knew about alchemy through his interest in the works of Théodore Flournoy and his contact with Hans Silberer. A psychoanalyst in the Vienna Circle, Silberer had been researching alchemy from the first decade of the twentieth century and Jung knew of his and Flournoy's work, both of which were interested in the psychological aspects of the subject. Silberer wrote a range of works on the occult arts from a psychoanalytic point of view. The most interesting of these was *Problems of Mysticism and its Symbolism* (1917). While writing *Transformations and Symbols of the Libido (Symbols of Transformation)* in 1912, Jung makes his first reference to alchemy, comparing an image of the process of cooking produced by a patient to the visions of the alchemist Zozimos of Panopolis (Shamdasani, 2012b, p. 167). Silberer had a rather reductionist bias, and explored alchemy and the occult arts (the expression used in the title of one of his books) from the psycho-analytic perspective of sublimation and the defences against repressed content. At the time, Jung did not thoroughly explore the symbolic source of alchemy. The subject appears throughout *Liber Novus*, how-ever, mainly within the theme of the bringing together of opposites (*coniunctio*), considered to be the final and most important alchemical operation (Jung discusses the profound significance of the *coniunctio* in alchemy in *Mysterium Coniunctionis* (1955)). We see this symbolism of opposites in images of black and white snakes and of night time and daylight, among others. But the most impressive alchemical symbol appears as Illustration 115 in Chapter 17 of *Liber Secundus*, "Nox Quarta" (Fourth Night). Jung illustrates a figure in black wearing a hat. It is in a type of closed cubicle with a black and white quadrangular floor. Jung wrote to the side of this illustration, "This is the golden fabric in which the shadow of God lives". The concept of golden fabric and the metals as being inhabited by the planetary gods is an ancient alchemical idea from the age of Alexander the Great.[7] The gods come down from the planets and develop within metals deep inside the earth. A network is created between the planets, the metals and the gods. The psychol-ogy of ancient man was intertwined with the environment and based on a web of significant connections. These appear again in the uncon-scious material of contemporary man. Alchemy is a hylozoistic tradi-tion in which the spiritual and the material (from the Greek *hylé*) are interwoven.[8] In alchemy, the world is not created by a demiurge, as the spiritual is not superior to the material, and the former has recovered its dignity from the great original mother. This unique cosmology may have been the main reason that Jung used alchemy as the principal ref-erence for his work after *Liber Novus*.

In the fragment cited there is a clear reference to alchemy. If Jung already knew about alchemy, his discovery of the alchemical treatise would not have been sufficient for him to abandon the writing of *Liber Novus*. We may suppose, however, that fewer unconscious images were appearing at that time in comparison to the key years of 1914–1917. The stormy waters were starting to calm. The rich symbolism from this period was gradually integrated into Jung's creative process over the years that followed. Shamdasani says that the assimilation of these experiences followed a non-linear, spiral process.[9] In subsequent work, the content of *Liber Novus* that emerged in confusing and meaningless symbols was gradually included in a consistent theoretical system. In his work, *the Relations between the Ego and Unconscious* (1928) Jung already mentioned "a technique of differentiation between the ego and the figures of the unconscious", and in the 1917 essay *The Structure of the Unconscious*, Jung talks about "attempts to free individuality from the collective psyche".[10] In *Psychological Types* (1921), the encounter with Elijah and Salome undergoes a sophisticated theoretical elaboration. In fact, all of the theory that Jung developed after this book derived from these seminal experiences: the understanding of the myth of totality in order to realise the personality, the criticism of empty institutional religion, the multicultural approach that is essential to modern times, and the model of the archetype in order to articulate his entire theoretical vision.

But did the continuous development of *The Red Book* stop at any point?

Shamdasani (2009) considered the construction of the Bollingen Tower with its mysterious inscriptions a continuation of the book, or in other words a true *Liber Quartus*. The work on this unique and revolutionary book was never truly abandoned. It was continued in various ways, and emerged in the author's theoretical works until the end of his life.

NOTES

Chapter One

1. Introduction to *The Red Book* by Ulrich Hoerni, president of the Foundation of the Works of C. G. Jung (previously the Society of Heirs of C. G. Jung).
2. Statistics provided by the Philemon Foundation on *The Red Book* can be found on the International Association for Analytical Psychology website: www.iaap.org.

Chapter Two

1. For more on the importance of childhood dreams see Jung, 1963.
2. For more on the importance of comparative mythological studies for Jung and psychoanalysis at the beginning of the twentieth century see Shamadasani, 2003, pp. 157–158.
3. For more on the origin of the name Abraxas and the characteristics of this deity see Mackay in Hoeller, 1982, p. 132.

Chapter Three

1. Jung divided *The Red Book* into two parts: *Liber Primus* and *Liber Secundus*. There is also a third part, *Scrutinies*, which Shamdasani calls *Liber Tertius* and which includes the active imaginations that were not included in the original manuscripts as well as the *Seven Sermons to the Dead*.

2. *Katabasis*: in the mystery religions of the ancient world, the novice always had to descend into the underworld and re-emerge transformed. The central archetypical mystery of *katabasis* can also be seen within the contemporary analytical process in the form of therapeutic regression.

3. The predominant belief system in Pharaonic Egypt involved the existence of various personified souls in the form of subtle bodies. The *Ba* is one of these bodies, which takes the form of a bird and represents the nucleus of the personality, the divine spark. This is different to the *Ka* soul, a subtle double personifying a person's vitality (Hannah, *Encounters with the Soul: Active Imagination as Developed by C. G. Jung*, 1981, pp. 85–86).

4. The Zofingia Club—A group to which Jung belonged while he was studying medicine at university. The members met regularly to hold conferences and debates on themes of culture and science. Jung's participation as a lecturer has been collated in a volume attached to his *Collected Works*, known as *Volume A, The Zofingia Lectures*, which includes an introduction by Marie-Louise von Franz.

5. It should be emphasised that Jung modifies, expands and corrects his comments on the direct perceptions of his fantasies on the second of the two "levels" of *The Red Book*. The fantasies and imaginations themselves were not altered.

6. Cultural evolutionism—An anthropological perspective from the nineteenth century adopted by Tylor, Frazer, Lévy-Brühl and others, by which European culture was seen as the ideal form of civilisation and tribal cultures as needing to develop to achieve the same model. The concept of pre-logical thinking (the mythological thinking of tribal societies being pre-logical and naturally inferior to the rational thinking of modernity) is an example of cultural evolutionism, a perspective that anthropologists now see as outdated.

Chapter Four

1. For more on how the *little dark man* character influenced Jung's research on the Trickster archetype while analyzing the anthropologist Paul

Radin's research into North-American Winnebago Indians (Jung, 1954a), see Shamdasani's notes on page 242 of *The Red Book* (Jung, 2009).

2. Joseph Henderson (1968) wrote about the various cycles of the trickster hero among the Native Americans. The trickster often takes the form of an animal, as seen in the cycle of the hare or the coyote. This is very different to the idealised hero of Germanic cycles.

3. Jung's dangerous proximity to Nazism is a complex issue containing various nuances and has been examined in great detail. One important text on this matter is Aniela Jaffé's *From the Life and Work of C. G. Jung* (1972), in the chapter entitled "C. G. Jung and National Socialism".

4. When treating Anna, Freud laid the foundations for a new method that would later be named psychoanalysis. Anna O. referred to Freud's method using metaphors such as "chimney-sweeping" and the "talking cure".

Chapter Five

1. This character has some connections with the epic poem "The Song of Hiawatha" by the North American poet Longfellow, quoted by Miss Miller herself, and dies when the ground gives way and a serpent attacks his arm and then his horse.

2. The conceptualisation of abnormal psychological symptoms is not easy. Firstly, the terms used in the American (DSM-5) and WHO (ICD-10) traditional medical classifications have been criticised as unable to provide an adequate overview of psychic suffering. The attempt to name extremely abnormal psychic states has also been criticised. Professor Ilídio Costa, coordinator of the Group for Early Intervention in Initial Psychotic Crises (GPSI) at the University of Brasília in Brazil proposes that a new approach be used for initial psychiatric crises. He suggests that the term "state of psychic suffering" is used, avoiding other names for serious psychological alterations that hinder the subject's full adaptation. This is a radical criticism of the incapacity of contemporary classification and diagnosis systems to describe the phenomena of the soul (Ribeiro, 2011, p. 71).

3. Incubation: from the Latin *cubare* "to lie down". Incubation dreams were old dream rituals used for healing purposes in the temples of Asclepius, the god of medicine, in Epidaurus, Dodona, and other shrines. See C. A. Meier, *Ancient Incubation and Modern Psychotherapy*. See also Jung's comparison of incubation dreams in *Liber Secundus*, Chapter 17: "Nox Quarta", p. 302.

4. This interpretation of the serpent as a representation of salvation comes from the Gnostic sects of the *Ofitas* group—the "serpent adorers".

5. The Sphinx's enigma is simple: "What animal is that which in the morning goes on four feet, at noon on two, and in the evening upon three?" Oedipus responds in a rational and simple way and believes he has solved it. Enigmas had a special importance in Ancient Greece. The Greek *aenigma* means "riddle" or "obscure saying". Enigmas were always present during wedding rituals and appeared in Hesiod's *Theogony* in the repeated theme of the primordial fathers and divine generations. Gaia (the lady of the oracles) always predicted to the Father God that his son would succeed and dethrone him. The Father God (Uranus, Cronus) prefers to destroy his son—committing filicide—trying to solve the enigma. Laius, by ordering the servant to kill the newborn Oedipus, follows the same mythical paradigm.

6. For more on the correlation between historical myths and Jung's personal myth see Shamdasani, 2007.

Chapter Six

1. For a comparison of Hegelian philosophy with the concept of the transcendent function see Solomon, 2011.

2. For more on the study of symbolic images produced by the unconscious in an analysis of dreams see Jung, 1964 and Jung, 1950.

3. For more on the verbs of the active imagination process see Humbert, 2004. Humbert suggests just the last three verbs. I suggest the first, "to empty", is usually necessary in order to carry out this process.

4. For more on James Hillman's term "polymorphous creative child" as a contrast to Freud's term "polymorphous perverse child" see Hillman, 1975. Hillman refers to the child's potential for creativity, which makes him an important symbol of the self.

5. *Bricolage* is a French word referring to automatic work using the hands involving creative expression and with no specific end. It describes playing or "daydreaming" with the hands.

6. Rather significantly, Dora Kaff (1980) claimed that she based her sand tray technique on the games that Jung played with small figures and sand on the banks of Lake Zurich during the time he was confronting his unconscious.

7. For more on the clinical cases cited see Boechat, 2009.

Chapter Seven

1. A heretical sect from the beginning of the fifteenth century that criticised the baptism of children and held that only adults should be baptised.
2. For more on the various rituals for the deceased in Brazil, see Cascudo's *Dicionário do Folclore Brasileiro* ("Dictionary of Brazilian Folklore"), s.v. *"alma"* (soul).
3. For more on this interpretation of the dead see the video by Murray Stein, "The Red Book of C. G. Jung", Ashville Center.
4. See Murray Stein's comments in the video from the Ashville Centre.
5. For more on Jung's doctorate thesis, *On the Psychology and Psychopathology of So-Called Occult Phenomena*, see Jung, 1902.
6. See *The Boundless Expanse: Jung's Reflection on Death and Life* (Shamdasani, 2007), a reference to how Jung referred to life after death experiences in *Archetypes of the Collective Unconscious*.
7. For more on investigations into mediums by the founders of psychology see Shamdasani, 1994, where he describes his revolutionary experiences with the medium Hélène Smith.
8. The diagnosis of somnambulism had an important role in psychopathological studies at the time as it explained altered states of consciousness. *Glossolalia* is a psychiatric term that describes when patients speak in a strange or uncommonly used language.

Chapter Eight

1. For more examples of mandalas used by the Navajo Indians and in Christianity see Jung, 1968b.
2. The ARAS can be visited by appointment at various Jungian Psychology Institutes throughout the United States: The C. G. Jung Institute of New York, The C. G. Jung Institute of Los Angeles, The C. G. Jung Institute of San Francisco and The C. G. Jung Institute of Chicago. The ARAS also has a comprehensive website at www.aras.org.
3. Expressions can be observed in various languages that describe the primary emotions outside the ego's control at a low level of consciousness that appear at the level of the stomach. For example, "to get butterflies in one's stomach" in English, and in Brazil, *"senti um frio no estômago"* (I felt a chill in my stomach).
4. For an overview of the psychological approach to the chakras see Jung, 1999.

5. More on the *Systema Munditotius* can be found in Appendix A of *Liber Novus* (Jung, 2009). According to Shamdasani, these descriptions of the mandala were given by Jung in a letter dated February 1955.

6. This god Eros is not related to the Eros described by Ovid in *Metamorphoses*, the mischievous winged boy who provokes mayhem with his arrows of love. The Orphics worship Eros *Protogenes*, which means in their cosmogony "the first-born" god who created the world.

7. For a detailed description of Orphism as a historical religious movement see Brandão, 1986 and 1991, Willi, 1944, and Graves, 1958.

8. From the Greek *metempsicosis*: the belief in reincarnation in any living body, whether animal, plant, or human. This differs from *ensomatosis*, the cycle of reincarnation restricted to human bodies. The Orphics professed metempsychosis.

9. "To take a step back in order to take a better jump"—a French expression used a lot by Jung in his studies into the psychodynamics of the neuroses. When faced with a problem, it is better to take a step back in order to jump and overcome it. This image can also be applied to the huge cultural changes that Europe was facing while *The Red Book* was being written. Modernity, for Jung, represented a range of problems and difficulties (the First World War being a very clear manifestation of these) and a step back to the past in search of references was required in order to find the solutions to these problems.

Chapter Nine

1. For more on the etymology of the word guru, see Wikipedia: www.wikipedia.org "Guru".

2. More on Izdubar chanting the Vedic mantras to restore virility to the sick, as well as this chapter's Hindu-inspired illustrations, can be seen in Chapter 10 of *Liber Secundus*, "The Incantations".

3. Joseph Campbell studied the image of a human figure with wings on the ancient route to the East from Rome to China and attributed the presence of wings to a Western influence in Eastern art. Wings are typical attributes of Western deities. See the video DVD *The Power of Myth*.

4. For more on the figure and symbolism of Ka, see Shamdasani's footnotes on pp. 305, 231, and 232 of *The Red Book*.

5. This term originates from alchemy. Jung uses it in the sense of circling a symbolic representation without reducing it to a single meaning. This is how he tries to respect mysterious unrepresented content.
6. Jung's description of the representation of Ka and Philemon can be found on p. 177 of *Memories, Dreams, Reflections.*

Chapter Ten

1. For more on the convergence of cultural production in 1906, see Stephen Martin, *Meaning in Art* (1990).
2. Dadaism was a cultural movement started by intellectuals in strong opposition to the ruling rationalism in Europe at the time. It originated in Zurich in 1916 and its main proponents were Tristan Tzara, Hugo Ball, and Hans Arp. *Dada* literally means "little wooden horse" or can represent the babbling of the first sounds made by a child (although the real significance of the name has never been discovered). For more on Dadaism as a reference to the situation in Europe at the time that *Liber Novus* was being written, see Shamdasani's introduction to *The Red Book.*
3. For more on the cultural significance of Monte Veritá and its main representatives see Martin Green, 1986.
4. The boundaries between the structure (the brain) *vs.* processes (the mind) in neuroscience are discussed by Damásio, 2010, and Capra, 2011, among other authors.
5. Jung reflects on the presence of the conscious in the unconscious—and the unconscious in the conscious—in *On the Nature of the Psyche* (1954b) using metaphors from the world of alchemy to elaborate on this matter, introducing Paracelsus's *lumen naturae*—the light of nature—and the shining eyes of fish at the bottom of the ocean.
6. For more on polarisations in the present-day paradigm see Sousa Santos, 2000, p. 90, in particular note 24.
7. For more on the legend of the descent of the planetary gods and the metals see *Alchemy, the Process of Individuation, Vols 1 and 2* (Jung, 1960 and Eliade, 1979).
8. For more on the concept of hylozoism see *Alchemy: The Process of Individuation* (Jung, 1960).
9. For more on the spiralled way in which Jung placed the experiences described in *Liber Novus* into his theories, see the interview that Shamdasani gave to Anne Casement (Casement, 2010).

10. The conference *The Structure of the Unconscious* was originally given in 1916, at the time of the author's experiences with *Liber Novus*. In this, Jung talks about attempts to free the individuality from the collective psyche. This conference would lead to the book *The Relations between the Ego and the Unconscious* (1928). In this there is a chapter called "The Technique of Differentiation between the Ego and the Figures of the Unconscious". This was clearly directly influenced by the experiences in *Liber Novus*.

REFERENCES

Alighieri, D. (1980). *The Divine Comedy*. Sao Paulo, Brazil: Círculo do Livro.

Armstrong, K. (2005). *A Short Story of Myth*. New York: Canongate.

Bachelard, G. (1989). *A poética do espaço*. Rio de Janeiro, Brazil: Martins Fontes.

Boechat, W. (2009). *A mitopoese da Psique: Mito e individuação (2nd edn.)*. Petropolis, Brazil: Vozes.

Bornheim, G. (Ed.) (2002). *Os filósofos pré-socráticos*. Sao Paulo, Brazil: Cultrix.

Brandão, J. (1986). *Mitologia Grega (Vol. I)*. Petropolis, Brazil: Vozes.

Brandão, J. (1987). *Mitologia Grega (Vol. III)*. Petropolis, Brazil: Vozes.

Brandão, J. (1991). *Dicionário Mítico-Etimológico da Mitologia Grega*. Petropolis, Brazil: Vozes.

Capra, F. (2011). *A Teia da Vida*. Sao Paulo, Brazil: Cultrix.

Cardoso, H. (1995). O mito do graal: resposta para a busca do homem moderno. In: W. Boechat (Ed.), *Mitos e Arquétipos do Homem Contemporâneo (2nd edn.)* (pp. 75–96). Rio de Janeiro, Brazil: Vozes.

Cascudo, C. (No date). *Dicionário do Folclore Brasileiro*. Sao Paulo, Brazil: Tecnoprint.

Casement, A. (2010). Sonu Shamdasani interviewed by Ann Casement. *Journal of Analytical Psychology, 55*: 35–39.

Chodorow, J. (1986). The body as symbol: Dance/movement in analysis. In: M. Stein (Ed.), *The Body in Analysis* (pp. 87–108). Wilmette, IL: Chiron.

Chodorow, J. (2008). *Dance Therapy and Depth Psychology: The Moving Imagination*. New York: Routledge.

da Matta, R. (1978). *Carnavais, Malandros e Heróis: Para uma Sociologia do Dilema Brasileiro (4th edn.)*. Rio de Janeiro, Brazil: Zahar.

Damasio, A. (2010). *Self Comes into Mind: Constructing the Conscious Brain* (Amazon Kindle edition). New York: Pantheon.

de la Rochefoucauld, F. (No date). *Reflections; or Sentences and Moral Maxims* (Amazon Kindle edition). A Public Domain Book.

Dourley, J. P. (1990). Jung's impact on religious studies. In: K. Barnaby & P. D'Acierno (Eds.), *C. G. Jung and the Humanities: Towards a Hermeneutics of Culture*. Princeton, NJ: Princeton University Press.

Drob, S. (2012). *Reading The Red Book. An Interpretive Guide to C. G. Jung's Liber Novus*. New Orleans, LA: Spring.

Edinger, E. (1996). *The Aion Lectures. Exploring the Self in C. G Jung's Aion*. Toronto, Canada: Inner City.

Eliade, M. (1962). *Patanjali et le Yoga*. Paris: Édition Du Seil.

Eliade, M. (1979). *The Forge and the Crucible (2nd edn)*. S. Corrin (Trans.). Chicago, IL: University of Chicago Press.

Eliade, M. (1983). *História das Crenças e das Idéias Religiosas: Da Idade da Pedra aos Mistérios de Elêusis (Volume 1)*. Rio de Janeiro, Brazil: Zahar.

Ellenberger, H. (1974). *À la Découverte de L`inconscient. Histoire de la Psiquiatrie Dynamique*. Villeurbanne, France: Simép.

Erasmus, D. (1511). *Éloge de la Folie*. Brussels: Ultraletters, 2013.

Flournoy, T. (1900). *From India to the Planet Mars: A Case of Multiple Personality with Imaginary Languages* (Introduction by Sonu Shamdasani). Princeton, NJ: Princeton University Press, 1994.

Freud, S. (1916–1917). *Introductory Lectures on Psycho-Analysis. S. E., 15–16*. London: Hogarth.

Freud, S. (1937c). Analysis terminable and interminable. *S. E., 23*. London: Hogarth.

Giegerich, W. (2008). *Liber Novus*, That is, The New Bible: A First Analysis of C. G. Jung's *Red Book. Spring: A Journal of Archetype and Culture, 83*: 361–441.

Graves, R. (1958). *Greek Myths*. London: Cassell.

Green, M. (1986). *Mountain of Truth: The Counterculture Begins. Ascona 1900–1920*. Hanover, NH: University Press of New England.

Hannah, B. (1981). *Encounters with the Soul: Active Imagination as Developed by C. G. Jung*. Boston, MA: Sigo Press.

Hauptmann, G. (1918). *O Herege de Soana*. A. Meyer (Trans.). Sao Paulo, Brazil: Delta, 1963.

Hayman, R. (2002). *A Life of Jung*. London: Bloomsbury.

Henderson, J. (1968). Ancient myths and modern man. In: C. G. Jung (Ed.), *Man and His Symbols*. New York: Random House.

Hillman, J. (1975). Abandoning the child. In: *Loose Ends. Primary Papers in Archetypal Psychology*. Zurich: Spring Publications.

Hillman, J. (1980). *Facing the Gods*. Dallas, TX: Spring Publications.

Hillman, J. (1983). *Healing Fiction*. Barrytown, NY: Station Hill.

Hillman, J., & Shamdasani, S. (2013). *Lament of the Dead: Psychology after Jung's Red Book*. New York: W. W. Norton.

Hoeller, S. (1982). *The Gnostic Jung and the Seven Sermons to the Dead*. Wheaton, IL: Quest.

Hölderlin, F. (1984). *Hymns and Fragments*. R. Sieburth. (Intro. & Trans.). Princeton, NJ: Princeton University Press.

Humbert, E. G. (2004). *Jung*. Paris: Hachette Littérature.

Jacoby, M. (1984). *The Analytical Encounter: Transference and Human Relationship*. Toronto, Canada: Inner City Books.

Jaffé, A. (1972). *From the Life and Work of C. G. Jung*. London: Hodder & Stoughton.

Jaffé, A. (Ed.) (1979). *C. G. Jung: Word and Image*. Princeton, NJ: Princeton University Press.

Jung, C. G. (1902). *On the Psychology and Psychopathology of the So-Called Occult Phenomena (2nd edn.). C. W., Volume 1*. Princeton, NJ: Princeton University Press, 1970.

Jung, C. G. (1911). *Symbols of Transformation (2nd edn., 1951, revised and expanded). C. W., Volume 5*. Princeton, NJ: Princeton University Press, 1956.

Jung, C. G. (1917). *The Structure of the Unconscious (2nd edn.). C. W., Volume 7*. Princeton, NJ: Princeton University Press, 1966.

Jung, C. G. (1921). *Psychological Types. C. W., Volume 6*. Princeton, NJ: Princeton University Press, 1970.

Jung, C. G. (1928). *The Relations between the Ego and the Unconscious. C. W., Volume 7*. Princeton, NJ: Princeton University Press, 1966.

Jung, C. G. (1931). *The Spiritual Problem of Modern Man (2nd edn.). C. W., Volume 10*. Princeton, NJ: Princeton University Press, 1970.

Jung, C. G. (1945). *Psychology and Alchemy (2nd edn.). C. W., Volume 12*. Princeton, NJ: Princeton University Press, 1968.

Jung, C. G. (1948a). *A Psychological Approach to the Dogma of the Trinity*. (2nd edn) C. W. *Volume 11*. Princeton, NJ: Princeton University Press, 1969.

Jung, C. G. (1948b). *The Phenomenology of the Spirit in Fairy Tales. C. W., Volume 9-1*. Princeton, NJ: Princeton University Press, 1959.

Jung, C. G. (1950a). *A Study in the Process of Individuation. C. W., Volume 9-1*. Princeton, NJ: Princeton University Press, 1959.

Jung, C. G. (1950b). *Concerning Mandala Symbolism. C. W., Volume 9-1.* Princeton, NJ: Princeton University Press, 1959.

Jung, C. G. (1951). *Aion. Researches into the Phenomenology of the Self. C. W., Volume 9-2.* Princeton, NJ: Princeton University Press, 1959.

Jung, C. G. (1952a). *Answer to Job (2nd edn.). C. W., Volume 11.* Princeton, NJ: Princeton University Press, 1969.

Jung, C. G. (1952b). *Synchronicity: An Acausal Connecting Principle (2nd edn.). C. W., Volume 8.* Princeton, NJ: Princeton University Press, 1969.

Jung, C. G. (1954a). *The Psychology of the Trickster Figure. C. W., Volume 9-1.* Princeton, NJ: Princeton University Press, 1959.

Jung, C. G. (1954b). *On the Nature of the Psyche (2nd edn.). C. W., Volume 8.* Princeton, NJ: Princeton University Press, 1969.

Jung, C. G. (1955). *Mysterium Coniunctionis (2nd edn.). C. W., Volume 14.* Princeton, NJ: Princeton University Press, 1970.

Jung, C. G. (1957). *Commentary on The Secret of the Golden Flower. C. W., Volume 13.* Princeton, NJ: Princeton University Press, 1967.

Jung, C. G. (1958). *The Transcendent Function (2nd edn.). C. W., Volume 8.* Princeton, NJ: Princeton University Press, 1969.

Jung, C. G. (1960). *Alchemy: the Process of Individuation. Vols 1, 2.* Notes on lectures given at the Eidgenössische Technische Hochschule, Zurich. November 1940–July 1941. Zurich: Karl Schippert.

Jung, C. G. (1963). *Memories, Dreams, Reflections.* A. Jaffé (Ed.). London: Collins and Routledge & Kegan Paul.

Jung, C. G. (1983). *The Zofingia Lectures. C. W., Volume A.* Princeton, NJ: Princeton University Press.

Jung, C. G. (1999). *The Psychology of Kundalini Yoga.* Notes on a seminar given in 1932. S. Shamdasani (Ed.). Princeton, NJ: Princeton University Press.

Jung, C. G. (2007). *The Jung-White Letters.* A. Conrad Lammers & A. Cunningham (Eds.), M. Stein (Consulting Ed.). Philemon series. New York: Routledge.

Jung, C. G. (2008). *Children's Dreams: Notes from the Seminar given in 1936–1940.* Philemon series. Princeton, NJ: Princeton University Press.

Jung, C. G. (2009). *The Red Book: Liber Novus.* S. Shamdasani (Ed. & Intro.). New York: W. W. Norton.

Jung, C. G. (2012). *Analytical Psychology: Notes on a Seminar given in 1925 by C. G. Jung.* W. McGuire (Intro.). Revised edition. S. Shamdasani (Intro.). Philemon series. Princeton, NJ: Princeton University Press.

Jung, C. G. (2014). *Dream Interpretation: Ancient and Modern. Notes on a Seminar given in 1936–1941.* Philemon series. Princeton, NJ: Princeton University Press.

Jung, C. G., & von Franz, M.-L. (Eds.) (1964). *Man and His Symbols.* New York: Random House, 1968.

Jung, E., & von Franz, M.-L. (1971). *The Grail Legend*. A. Dyckes (Trans.). London: Hodder & Stoughton.

Kalff, D. (1980). *Sandplay: A Psychotherapeutic Approach to the Psyche*. Santa Monica, CA: Sigo Press.

Kalsched, D. (2013). *Trauma and the Soul*. London: Routledge.

Khun, T. (1962). *The Structure of Scientific Revolutions*. Chicago, IL: University of Chicago Press.

Martin, S. (1990). Meaning in art. In: K. Barnaby & P. D'Acierno (Eds.), *C. G. Jung and the Humanities: Towards a Hermeneutics of Culture*. Princeton, NJ: Princeton University Press.

Meier, C. A. (1967). *Ancient Incubation and Modern Psychotherapy*. Evanston, IL: Northwestern University Press.

Morin, E. (1999). Por uma reforma do pensamento. In: A. Pena-Vega & E. Nascimento (Eds.), *O Pensar Complexo*. Rio de Janeiro, Brazil: Garamond.

Paris, G. (1986). *Pagan Meditations. The Worlds of Aphrodite, Atermis and Hestia*. Dallas, TX: Spring Publications.

Perry, J. W. (1974). *The Far Side of Madness*. Upper Saddle River, NJ: Prentice Hall.

Radin, P. (1972). *The Trickster: A Study in American Indian Mythology* (with commentary by K. Kerényi and C. G. Jung). New York: Schocken.

Ribeiro, P. (2011). Primeiras crises psíquicas graves e a typelogia de Jung: um estudo exploratório. Master's thesis presented for the postgraduate program in clinical psychology at the University of Brasilia.

Rosa, G. (1963). *The Devil to Pay in the Backlands*. J. L. Taylor & H. de Onís (Trans.). (Preface by Jorge Amado.) New York: Knopf.

Servant-Schreiber, D. (2007). *Anticancer. Prevenir et lutter grâce à nos défenses naturelles*. Paris: Robert Laffond.

Shamdasani, S. (1990). A woman called Frank. *Spring, An Annual of Archetypal Psychology and Jungian Thought, 50*: 26–56.

Shamdasani, S. (1994). Encountering Hélène: Theodore Flournoy and the genesis of subliminal psychology. In: T. Flournoy (Ed.), *From India to the Planet Mars: A Case of Multiple Personality with Imaginary Languages*. Princeton, NJ: Princeton University Press.

Shamdasani, S. (1995). Memories, dreams, omissions. *Spring, An Annual of Archetypal Psychology and Jungian Thought, 57*: 115–137.

Shamdasani, S. (2003). *Jung and the Making of Modern Psychology—The Dream of a Science*. Cambridge: Cambridge University Press.

Shamdasani, S. (2005). *Jung Stripped Bare: By his Biographers, Even*. London: Karnac.

Shamdasani, S. (2007). The Boundless Expanse: Jung's reflection on death and life (Conference by the Jungian Psychoanalytical Association (JPA),

New York, on November 2. Text provided by the author to the Jungian Institute of Rio Grande do Sul, Brazil.

Shamdasani, S. (2009). Liber Novus: The Red Book of C. G. Jung. In: C. G. Jung (Ed.), *The Red Book. Liber Novus*. New York: W. W. Norton.

Shamdasani, S. (2012a). After Liber Novus. *Journal of Analytical Psychology*, 57: 364–377.

Shamdasani, S. (2012b). *C. G. Jung: A Biography in Books*. New York: W. W. Norton (in association with the Martin Bodmer Foundation).

Silberer, H. (1917). *Hidden Symbolism of Alchemy and the Occult Arts (Problems of Mysticism and its Symbolism)*. New York: Dover (1971).

Silveira, N. (1980). *A Esquizofrenia em Imagens*. Rio de Janeiro, Brazil: Alhambra.

Solomon, H. (2011). Ethics and Jungian Analysis. In: M. Stein (Ed.), *Jungian Psychoanalysis* (Amazon Kindle Edition).

Sousa Santos, B. (2000). *A Crítica da Razão Indolente: Contra o Desperdício da Experiência* (2nd Edn). Sao Paulo, Brazil: Cortez.

Von Franz, M. L. (1975). *C. G. Jung: His Myth in Our Time*. New York: C. G. Jung Foundation for Analytical Psychology.

Willi, W. (1944). The Orphic Mysteries and the Greek Spirit. In: *The Mysteries. Papers from the Eranos Yearbooks, 2*. Princeton, NJ: Princeton University Press [reprinted in 1971].

Winnicott, D. W. (1989). Review of Memories, Dreams, Reflections. In: C. Winnicott, R. Shepherd, & M. Davis (Eds.), *Psychoanalytical Explorations* (pp. 482–492). Cambridge, MA: Harvard University Press.

Electronic documents

Everett, Derrick (2011)—Monsalvat: The Parsifal home page. http://www.monsalvat.no/kundry.htm. Accessed on January 12, 2012.

Videos consulted

Brutsche, Paul, & Stein, Murray—*Windows of the Soul*. DVD. Ashville Center.

Campbell, Joseph—*The Power of Myth*. Collection of four DVDs.

Hillman, James—*Images of the Soul*. Lecture at Pacifica Institute. DVD.

Stein, Murray—*The Red Book of C. G. Jung*. 2 DVDs. Ashville Center.

INDEX

Printed in Great Britain
by Amazon

54144846R00090